You Could Die Laughing!

A Murder Mystery/Comedy

by Billy St. John

A SAMUEL FRENCH ACTING EDITION

FOUNDED 1830
New York Hollywood London Toronto
SAMUELFRENCH.COM

Copyright © 2001, 2003 by Billy St. John

ALL RIGHTS RESERVED

CAUTION: Professionals and amateurs are hereby warned that *YOU COULD DIE LAUGHING!* is subject to a Licensing Fee. It is fully protected under the copyright laws of the United States of America, the British Commonwealth, including Canada, and all other countries of the Copyright Union. All rights, including professional, amateur, motion picture, recitation, lecturing, public reading, radio broadcasting, television and the rights of translation into foreign languages are strictly reserved. In its present form the play is dedicated to the reading public only.

The amateur live stage performance rights to *YOU COULD DIE LAUGHING!* are controlled exclusively by Samuel French, Inc., and licensing arrangements and performance licenses must be secured well in advance of presentation. PLEASE NOTE that amateur Licensing Fees are set upon application in accordance with your producing circumstances. When applying for a licensing quotation and a performance license please give us the number of performances intended, dates of production, your seating capacity and admission fee. Licensing Fees are payable one week before the opening performance of the play to Samuel French, Inc., at 45 W. 25th Street, New York, NY 10010.

Licensing Fee of the required amount must be paid whether the play is presented for charity or gain and whether or not admission is charged.

Stock licensing fees quoted upon application to Samuel French, Inc.

For all other rights than those stipulated above, apply to: Samuel French, Inc.

Particular emphasis is laid on the question of amateur or professional readings, permission and terms for which must be secured in writing from Samuel French, Inc.

Copying from this book in whole or in part is strictly forbidden by law, and the right of performance is not transferable.

Whenever the play is produced the following notice must appear on all programs, printing and advertising for the play: "Produced by special arrangement with Samuel French, Inc."

Due authorship credit must be given on all programs, printing and advertising for the play.

ISBN 978-0-573-62972-3

No one shall commit or authorize any act or omission by which the copyright of, or the right to copyright, this play may be impaired.

No one shall make any changes in this play for the purpose of production.

Publication of this play does not imply availability for performance. Both amateurs and professionals considering a production are *strongly* advised in their own interests to apply to Samuel French, Inc., for written permission before starting rehearsals, advertising, or booking a theatre.

No part of this book may be reproduced, stored in a retrieval system, or transmitted in any form, by any means, now known or yet to be invented, including mechanical, electronic, photocopying, recording, videotaping, or otherwise, without the prior written permission of the publisher.

IMPORTANT BILLING AND CREDIT REQUIREMENTS

All producers of YOU COULD DIE LAUGHING! *must* give credit to the Author of the Play in all programs distributed in connection with performances of the Play and in all instances in which the title of the Play appears for purposes of advertising, publicizing or otherwise exploiting the Play and/or a production. The name of the Author *must* appear on a separate line on which no other name appears, immediately following the title, and *must* appear in size of type not less than fifty percent the size of the title type.

CAST OF CHARACTERS

Mr. Thorn: 50's, gaunt, dour, doesn't say much
Mrs. Thorn: 50's, gaunt, dour, what she says is sharp and critical
Susan Harrison: 20's, pretty, a flight attendant
Allen Rudolph: 30's, handsome, a pilot
Corky Evans: 20's, a zany comic, does impersonations and funny voices
Zowie Miller: 20's, a savvy, modern, female comic
Lucinda Tate: 50's to 60's, loud clothes, loud mouth, does broad comedy
Helena Hollis: 30's, catty, sarcastic, but funny
Dexter Porter & Stanley: 50's, a ventriloquist and his little boy dummy
Antonio Johnson: 20's, a New York street-smart comic
Sammy Salt: 40's, plays straight man to his ditzy wife
Paulette Pepper: 40's, aforementioned ditzy wife
Joey James: 50 but looks 40, conceited, arrogant, can be cruel
Cora Apple: 40's or older, a country comedienne
Colleen Baker: 30's, a household hints expert who happens to be funny

SYNOPSIS OF SCENES

Time: The Present.
Place: Millionaire television mogul Jacque St. Yves' lodge
on a deserted island off the Canadian coastline.

ACT I
Scene 1: Friday morning. About 11:00 a.m.
Scene 2: Friday afternoon. About 5:00 p.m.
Scene 3: Friday night. About 8:00 p.m.

ACT II
Scene 1: Saturday morning. About 1:00 a.m.
Scene 2: Two hours later. About 3:00 a.m.

ACT I

Scene 1

(Friday morning. About 11:00 a.m.
The setting is the main room of a rustic, but attractive, lodge on a deserted island off the Canadian coastline. A stone fireplace is centered on the SR wall. A clock sits on the mantle. It has a pendulum and a glass door that opens to give access to the clock face and pendulum. It should actually work. It is set at 11:00 o'clock. A bench sits before the fireplace. A narrow platform spans UC, elevating the entry area. A front door with a glass pane in the upper half, which opens in, and a bay window are in the US wall. A window seat is built in below the window; the seat has a hinged lid which can be raised for storage space. A door at the SR end of the platform in the US corner of the SR wall opens out to a coat closet. A doorway at the opposite end of the platform in the US corner of the SL wall gives access to a corridor that leads to the bedrooms upstairs. A light switch is beside the doorway. A wide step joins the platform to the main room. Beyond the window is a backdrop that depicts a forest in the distance. DS in the SL wall is a swinging door that leads to the kitchen. There is a round games table with four low-back, wooden captain's chairs DR. A sofa with a coffee table below it sits DL. There are two matching chairs which swivel on either side of the coffee table, facing in. The decor can include bookcases, area rugs, a stuffed animal head over the fireplace, exposed beams from which could hang rustic chandeliers, and such. The room is attractive and reflects wealth.

6   YOU COULD DIE LAUGHING!

AT RISE: The stage is empty. There is the sound of a small jet plane which will grow in volume as it approaches. MR. THORN enters off UL to behind the window. MR. THORN is a dour, gaunt looking man, somewhat skeletal, with his hair combed slick against his skull. He wears work clothes, not especially clean. He is a man of few words and the ones he uses are said without a lot of emotion. You could say he appears somewhat sinister. He is carrying an armload of firewood. He stops behind the window and looks up, we presume at the landing plane. MRS. THORN enters DL from the kitchen. She is a female clone of her husband, sour and stern-faced. She wears a plain black dress and has her hair pulled back into a tight bun. Her words, when uttered, are sharp and critical. She is carrying two silver candy dishes in which are mints. She, too, listens a beat. The plane lands; its engine would will fade out. She crosses to the coffee table and sets a dish on it as MR. THORN crosses to the front door. He taps on it with his foot. MRS. THORN looks up and sees him, quickly sets the other dish on the round table DR, then crosses to the door and opens it. MR. THORN enters.)

MR. THORN. They're here, Mrs. Thorn.
MRS. THORN. I realize that, Mr. Thorn.
MR. THORN. Hands full.
MRS. THORN. Can see that. *(He starts toward the fireplace.)* Don't track dirt on the floor.
MR. THORN. 'Spect me to walk on the ceiling? *(He puts the wood into a holder on the hearth.)* Everything ready?
MRS. THORN. As it's going to be.
MR. THORN. Bathrooms?
MRS. THORN. Cleaned.
MR. THORN. Wash cloths and towels?
MRS. THORN. Fresh.
MR. THORN. Ham?
MRS. THORN. Baked. Firewood?
MR. THORN. Chopped.
MRS. THORN. Truck?

YOU COULD DIE LAUGHING!

MR. THORN. Gassed.
MRS. THORN. Rat poison?
MR. THORN. Set out. Just finished.
MRS. THORN. Good. You need to fetch the luggage. Come with me. *(She starts toward the door DL. He starts to follow, stops, and takes a mint from the bowl on the table DR. MRS. THORN stops and turns back toward him. He starts to put the mint into his mouth.)* Did you wash your hands after you handled the poison?

(He stops with the candy at his open mouth, hesitates, then starts to put it back into the dish. MRS. THORN makes a harsh grunt. MR. THORN hesitates, then puts the mint into his pants pocket. MRS. THORN nods at him, turns, and exits DL. MR. THORN follows her, brushing his hands on his pants, and exits. After a beat, we hear the sound of voices off UR. It grows until we see the passengers from the plane start to appear behind the front door. They ENTER. The group includes:

ALLEN RUDOLPH, the pilot, a handsome man in his 30's. He wears a pilot's uniform.
SUSAN HARRISON, the attendant, pretty, in her 20's. She wears a flight attendant's uniform.
CORA APPLE, 40's or older, a country comedienne. She wears a bright, old-fashioned looking dress of calico or gingham. She is loud and brash when performing, but quieter when not.
HELENA HOLLIS, a catty, sarcastic woman, in her 30's. She is well-groomed and dressed in a chic pants suit.
JOEY JAMES, a conceited, arrogant man who can be cruel. He is 50, but thanks to black hair dye and cosmetic surgery, he looks 40.

NOTE: in the scenes where it indicates that the comics react in a supportive manner to one another, JOEY will be the exception; he will simply smirk as if he thinks he's better than the rest.

DEXTER PORTER, a ventriloquist in his 50's or 60's, dressed in

a conservative suit. He carries his dummy, STANLEY, who wears a kid's outfit. It isn't important that the actor playing DEXTER be an accomplished ventriloquist as long as he creates a suitable humorous voice for STANLEY.
ANTONIO JOHNSON, a hip, New York street-wise comic in his 20's. His clothes are modern and funky.
CORKY EVANS, a wild comic who makes off-the-wall comments, does imitations, and comes out with weird noises. He is in his 20's and wears loud clothes, maybe plaid pants with a bright print shirt.
ZOWIE MILLER, a with-it, modern woman in her 20's. Her clothes are casual and comfortable, maybe baggy pants and a t-shirt.
LUCINDA TATE, a woman in her 50's or 60's. She has wild hair, wild clothes, and a wild sense of humor. She is loud and outgoing, and makes gags about her four ex-husbands.
SAMMY SALT & PAULETTE PEPPER are a couple in their 40's. He is the straight man of the act, and she is the ditzy partner. They are married in real life. He wears slacks, a sport coat and turtleneck shirt; she wears a dress.
COLLEEN BAKER, in her 30's, an expert on household hints who happens to be funny. She has a sunny disposition. She wears a summer dress with a full skirt, maybe a floral print.

All the guests wear or carry lightweight coats or jackets and carry purses and/or duffel bags and/or vanity kits. They spread out into the room and look around.)

ALLEN. Come in, everyone. *(He checks his watch and the mantle clock.)* Eleven o'clock. Right on schedule. The Thorns are here somewhere. They'll show you to your rooms.

CORKY. The Thorns?

ALLEN. They work for M. *("Monsieur")* St. Yves. Mr. Thorn is a handyman, and Mrs. Thorn will cook the meals while you're here. M. St. Yves has me fly the Thorns to the island ahead of time whenever he has guests here to get the lodge in order. I brought them last weekend.

ZOWIE. She's a cook, huh? That's good to know. Looking down from the air on all those woods, I was afraid lunch would be whatever I could catch with my bare hands.

LUCINDA. Really? I was thinking if there are bears or mountain lions out there, WE might end up being someTHING's lunch.

ZOWIE. Thanks for sharing that with us, Lucinda. Now I'm terrified to step out the front door. I hope they have indoor plumbing here, or I'm gonna be in real trouble!

(In the distance, we hear the sound of a truck engine starting; the motor noise will fade in the distance.)

ALLEN. *(Laughing.)* Don't worry, the lodge is fully equipped with all the modern conveniences ... and I promise you, there are lots of deer and raccoons and opossums on the island, but no man -- or lady -- eaters. You're all perfectly safe.

STANLEY (DEXTER). Oh, yeah? What about woodpeckers?

ALLEN. *(With a grin.)* We do have woodpeckers, uh ...?

DEXTER. This is Stanley. Stanley's greatest fear is woodpeckers ... next to termites, that is.

ANTONIO. Hey, no problemo, little guy. We can empty one of these candy bowls and tie it on top of your noggin.

CORKY. Good thinking, Antonio. That'd take care of the feathered fiends. *(He gives the Woody Woodpecker laugh as he bobs his head as if pecking.)* Ha-ha-ha-HA-ha ... *(He bends the tip of his nose down with a forefinger.)* ... ooowww!

ANTONIO. Good one, Corky.

JOEY. That's a matter of opinion.

ALLEN. You might keep an eye out for snakes, though. I saw a copperhead the last time I was here. Mr. Thorn shot and killed it with a pistol.

PAULETTE. Snakes! I'm scared of snakes!

SAMMY. Don't worry, Paulette. If we see a snake, I'll hand you a stick to fight it with while I run for help.

PAULETTE. Thank you, Sammy, dear. You're a good husband.

HELENA. As compared to what? None at all?

LUCINDA. Hey, I've got none at all, and I prefer it that way. I decided to call it quits after I had to put four husbands into the ground. Believe me, they didn't like that a bit!

PAULETTE. Was that a joke?

LUCINDA. If you have to ask, the answer is probably "no". It's a line I use in my routine. The part about having four ex-husbands is true. Unfortunately, they're still alive and kicking.

PAULETTE. You've had FOUR husbands!?! The only one I've ever had is Sammy. I didn't know you were supposed to trade them in!

LUCINDA. It's the same as with cars, Paulette — swap 'em only if you get a lemon. With each husband I thought "my cup runneth over with love", but it turned out to be lemonade.

ALLEN. I hope you still like it — lemonade, I mean. Mrs. Thorn usually serves lemonade with lunch.

SUSAN. Good.

LUCINDA. Oh, sure, I still have a taste for the stuff. Maybe that's why I keep getting married.

PAULETTE. *(Who has been concentrating.)* Husbands are like cars.... I get it. Well, after all the years we've been together, I might as well keep you, dear.

HELENA. Yeah — in case you see a snake.

SAMMY. And because she loves me.

(PAULETTE AND SAMMY kiss.)

SUSAN. That's sweet. You don't see many couples who stay together as long as Mr. Salt and Ms. Pepper have.

HELENA. It's sweet, all right — I'm getting a sugar rush just from watching them.

COLLEEN. Oh, Helena, you're just an old cynic.

HELENA. I resent that! I'm a young cynic, and I've built my career around it.

JOEY. For all the good it did you. *(HELENA shoots him a look.)* Hey, nothing personal — we're all in the same boat here.

YOU COULD DIE LAUGHING! 11

ANTONIO. You're mighty quiet, Cora ... which is real unusual. What gives?

CORA. *(With a strong country accent.)* Oh, I wuz just thinking how this place reminds me of my upbringing. My folks and us eight kids lived in a cabin in the Ozarks when I wuz a young'un. Not a fancy place like this, though. We didn't have no plumbing, just a crick.

ANTONIO. Outhouse?

CORA. Nearest bush.

COLLEEN. I bet your home was quaint. Quaint is in now, you know. This place is fabulous!

ZOWIE. The Queen of Interior Design has spoken! If Colleen Baker says it's so, it must be so!

COLLEEN. Well, it's my business to know these things, Zowie.

DEXTER. Colleen, if your interest is in homemaking, how did you ever end up in comedy?

CORKY. Yeah. How did you get into the business? I knew I wanted to be a comic ever since I was ten and got laughs from the other kids at school. I'd imitate our teacher, Mrs. Klinger, who was born in Germany and had this thick accent. *(Imitating her accent.)* "Boys und girls, you vill take out your pen-zils und paper und draw a picture of yourselves, yah-vole? Vhy, Corky — vhat is dot!?! Who do you tink you are, Picasso? Are doze your nostrils, or do you haf two sets of eyeballs? Dee-minus!"

(The others chuckle.)

STANLEY (DEXTER). As Dexter was saying before he was so humorously interrupted, how did YOU end up in comedy, Colleen?

COLLEEN. It was very strange. I was hired to tape a household hints show at a local TV station in Cleveland. On the first show, I told everyone how to prepare a cabbage casserole. Apparently, when I instructed everyone to boil their heads before sticking them into the oven, the viewers thought it was hilarious. We found out later they laughed at all my tips. The station owner said the switchboard lit up like Times Square on New Year's Eve from the calls that flooded in.

Before I knew it, I was doing "Colleen's Hilarious Household Hints." A year later, my show was picked up by NBC. Now I'm a comedy star ... at least I was for five years before the show was cancelled.

ANTONIO. We all know what that's like, baby. On minute I was number one in the ratings, the next I was bumped off the charts by a "reality crime stoppers" show. Hey, I'm an inner city kid. I stop crime all the time. All I do is lean out of my window and yell down, "Hey, you guys — stop that, ya hear?" At least your show ran five years — mine got the ax after two.

ZOWIE. *(Raising her hand.)* Mine ran two years — just barely. I knew casting me as a funny nun was a big mistake. You try to get laughs covered in a black sheet sometime.

(ZOWIE lowers her hand.)

SAMMY. *(Raising his hand.)* Three years for us.

(SAMMY raises PAULETTE's hand. DEXTER, CORKY and CORA raise theirs, then all five lower them.)

HELENA. *(Raising her hand.)* Seven. *(The others ad-lib comments like "Wow! I'm impressed!" HELENA lowers her hand.)* Joey?

JOEY. One, and don't start feeling superior. The producers had no idea how to use a talent like mine.

CORKY. *(A whisper to ANTONIO.)* On the contrary, I think they knew exactly how to use it — they canceled the big jerk.

ANTONIO. *(Whispering back.)* Uh-huh. *(Out loud.)* Lucinda?

LUCINDA. One, but I got a movie. *(The others make impressed noises.)* It laid an egg big enough to feed Pittsburgh.

(The others groan.)

ANTONIO. So we've all got two things in common: we're comics and we're all residents of "Has-Been City."

HELENA. But not for long — one of us will be on top again when Mr. St. Yves decides which one will star in the new TV series he's planning for his network — or two, if Sammy and Paulette are picked.

SUSAN. It's "Monsieur" St. Yves, Ms. Hollis. He's French-Canadian and is very touchy about his title.

HELENA. Thanks for the tip, Susan. I'll call him "your holiness" and kiss his ring if it gets me the job.

STANLEY (DEXTER). I'd kiss his feet but I might give him splinters.

DEXTER. Smart thinking, Stanley — and you might get athlete's lips.

STANLEY (DEXTER). That's true, Dexter. Besides, I'm still trying to figure out how to pucker.

PAULETTE. Now I remember ....

SAMMY. Remember what, dear?

PAULETTE. *(To DEXTER.)* I remember where I've seen you — on TV. You and your little boy. You look a little older, but he hasn't changed a bit.

DEXTER. That was a long time ago, Miss Pepper. The sponsor dropped "The Dexter Porter and Stanley Show" because he said we were too old-fashioned.

JOEY. He had a point.

CORKY. That's a lot of hooey, Joey! *(To DEXTER.)* You were funny, man. I watched you when I was a kid. I laughed my head off. *(He steps behind ANTONIO and sticks his head under ANTONIO's arm so that it looks as if ANTONIO is holding his disembodied head.)* Excuse me, have you seen my body? It was here just a moment ago.

ANTONIO. *(Releasing CORKY.)* Corky's right -- good comedy never goes out of style. You've still got it, Dexter.

DEXTER. Thank you, young fellas. I think that talent lasts forever.

STANLEY (DEXTER). Once a star, always a star. Right, Dexter?

DEXTER. Right, Stanley. *(To all.)* I'm certain there are people out there who still recognize me. When I'm in public places, I often sense that I'm being stared at.

SUSAN. I'm sure that's true, Mr. Porter ... and I'm sure you'll be a big TV star again.

JOEY. How much you want to bet on that?

ZOWIE. Can it, Joey! Susan's right! We've all got a shot at the prize! Look, gang, we've all been on top before, and we'll all be on top again, sooner or later. All we need is a second chance.

(The others, except JOEY, ad-lib agreement enthusiastically.)

DEXTER. *(To SUSAN.)* I've been wondering ... uh ... what's your name again?

SUSAN. It's Susan ... Susan Harrison.

DEXTER. Susan.... I've always like that name. In fact ....

STANLEY (DEXTER). *(Cutting in.)* There you go, rambling on, Dexter. Ask the young woman your question.

DEXTER. Yes, of course. I have to depend on Stanley to keep me on track sometime. What I was wondering is, when do we get to show M. St. Yves our acts?

JOEY. Soon, hopefully, before some of us become too senile to perform them.

(JOEY looks directly at DEXTER.)

SUSAN. Allen is supposed to fly him over the day after tomorrow — Sunday. He thought you might want some time to relax and maybe practice your routines for your auditions.

COLLEEN. I certainly want to make a good impression. I wouldn't have worn my best dress if I had know we wouldn't see him today. No problem, though — I'll turn on the shower until the bathroom steams up, then hang the dress on the shower rod. The steam will take out the wrinkles.

LUCINDA. Too bad it doesn't work on skin.

(We hear the sound of the truck approaching fade in, it will continue a few beats, then the engine will die, out back.)

HELENA. Since we're all from the States, we're not that familiar with M. St. Yves. What can you tell us about him?

ALLEN. He's very business-like — not what you'd call friendly, but he's always treated me fairly. Don't you agree, Susan?

SUSAN. Completely — stern, but fair.

HELENA. Oh, great. It sounds like our auditions are going to be as much fun as making a guest appearance at the Spanish Inquisition!

JOEY. Why don't you ask Dexter what that was like? I understand the Inquisition was his first gig.

HELENA. *(Sarcastic.)* Very funny, Joey. I happen to know Dexter's not all that much older than you are. The difference is, HE hasn't gone in for face lifts and hair dye.

(JOEY shoots her an angry glare.)

DEXTER. Thank you, Helena, dear.

STANLEY (DEXTER). We owe you one.

HELENA. Don't mention it. Allen, you were saying about M. St. Yves?

ALLEN. Don't worry if he doesn't laugh at your auditions — even if the man doesn't have a great sense of humor, he knows there's money to be made from comedy. He owns several very popular cable networks here in Canada.

SUSAN. Including *The Comedy Connection*. That's the channel he plans to develop the new series for — the one you're trying out for. I heard him tell an associate on the phone that he wants to develop it around the talents of a former comedy star. Nostalgia is in, he said.

CORKY. That's how my agent put it. *(The other comics ad-lib their agents did too.)* It's strange I haven't seen the new show mentioned in *Variety*, though.

SUSAN. Perhaps M. St. Yves wants to wait until it's cast and in production before he goes public with it.

COLLEEN. Well, whatever happens, at least we've got an all-expense paid trip to an attractive, if primitive, island off Canada.

CORA. Yore rite, Colleen. I'm gonna think of this trip as a nice weekend get-away whether I git the job or not.

LUCINDA. Me, too. This island is a paradise — nicer than where

I went on any of my honeymoons, which isn't saying much. Husband number two took me to the La Brea Tar Pits; that honeymoon was "the pits" in more ways than one. But M. St. Yves' beautiful island — what could possibly spoil it?

(As if to answer her question, MR. and MRS. THORN enter DL. He has a piece of luggage in each hand and one under each arm.)

    MRS. THORN. We're the Thorns.
    ANTONIO. *(Under his breath to ZOWIE.)* Did someone, like, order a pair of ghouls from Central Casting?
    ALLEN. These are all the guests, Mrs. Thorn.
    SUSAN. They're comedians. You might recognize some of them from their TV shows.
    MRS. THORN. Don't watch television.
    MR. THORN. Don't like it.
    ZOWIE. *(Under her breath to ANTONIO.)* Good thing they've never seen us. I bet if they cracked a smile, their faces would fall off.
    JOEY. *(Under his breath.)* In their case, it would be an improvement.
    MRS. THORN. Mr. Thorn has brought your luggage from the plane. I've prepared your rooms. *(To ALLEN and SUSAN.)* You're staying too?
    ALLEN. Just overnight, then Susan and I will fly back to the mainland tomorrow morning.
    MRS. THORN. *(Nods curtly.)* Follow us.

(The THORNS cross to the platform and head toward the archway UL. The others gather their items and follow. Bringing up the rear, CORKY — making fun of the THORNS — does a stiff-legged, arms-extended walk like Frankenstein's monster. When MRS. THORN stops at the archway, turns back and sees him, he quickly drops the imitation.)

    CORKY. Lumbago.

YOU COULD DIE LAUGHING! 17

MRS. THORN. Lunch will be served in one hour. If you're late, you'll have to fend for yourselves.

(MRS. THORN turns and goes through the archway. The others follow, muttering among themselves as they exit.)

HELENA. Who starched her girdle?
CORA. They ain't from the South, that's fer sure. T'ain't at all friendly. Didn't so much as say "Howdy."
HELENA. Or even "Kiss my grits."
STANLEY (DEXTER). Promise you won't leave me alone with that Mr. Thorn, Dexter. He looked at me like he was sizing me up for firewood.
DEXTER. I'll protect you, Stanley.
COLLEEN. I feel like a girl again, at a summer camp. I wish I had brought something to kill the mosquitoes with.
ZOWIE. I did.
COLLEEN. What?
ZOWIE. *(Holding out a hand.)* This. Works great. *(She smacks her own arm.)* Gets 'em every time.

(The lights fade to blackout as they exit.)

Scene 2

(That afternoon. About 5:00 p.m.
Once the cast has cleared offstage and a STAGEHAND has moved the clock hands to 4:50, the lights fade up. It is late afternoon; the light beyond the window is not as bright and the sky will become overcast as the scene progresses. In this scene, the cast will have removed their outerwear. After a beat, CORKY's head pops up behind the window. He is on his hands and knees, imitating a squirrel. His head drops back down and he scurries to the front door, raises up on his knees again, and grips a doorknob with

both "paws," opening it. He scurries in, still on hands and knees, and goes to SL of the table DR. He raises up, sniffs, wags his "tail" briskly, then takes a mint from the bowl with his "paws." He doesn't see ZOWIE enter UL. She stops and watches him. He puts the mint between his teeth, drops back down, and furiously mimes digging a hole in the floor.)

ZOWIE. Lose a contact lens?

(CORKY, startled, gasps and seemingly swallows and chokes on the mint. The effect is comical, though not intentional. ZOWIE crosses to him as he gets to his feet and regains his breath.)

CORKY. I wish you wouldn't do that, Zowie. I swallowed a mint. It stuck right here. *(He touches his neck.)* Now every time I breathe out, I become a walking Glade dispenser.

ZOWIE. Yeah, yeah.... If you don't mind my asking, what the heck were you doing?

CORKY. I took a walk in the woods. There's a bunch of squirrels out there.

ZOWIE. There's a bunch of squirrels in here.

CORKY. I mean the real kind, you know — with the chubby cheeks and bushy tails. I got the idea to maybe add a squirrel to my repertoire of characters. I was practicing burying a "nut" when you scared me out of a year's growth.

ZOWIE. You're tall enough already. Keep working on the character — you looked pretty funny.

CORKY. Thanks. I think one of the hardest things about being a comic is coming up with fresh material. Agree?

ZOWIE. Absolutely. I had a whole staff of writers for my TV show, but for my stand-up routine, I write my own jokes.

CORKY. Same here. I guess none of us ex-TV stars can afford to hire gag men at this stage of our careers.

ZOWIE. I'd say you got that right.

CORKY. Where is everybody, anyway?

ZOWIE. I took a nap after that huge lunch Mrs. Thorn set out. I think some of the others did too. I'll say one thing for Mrs. T — she might not be Miss Congeniality, but the woman sure can cook.

    CORKY. Yeah. I pigged out on the ham. "Hammed out on the pig"? There ought to be a joke there somewhere.

    ZOWIE. Keep looking, honey.

(DEXTER enters UL with STANLEY.)

    DEXTER. Ah, there are others stirring about, I see.
    CORKY. Hi, Dexter. What've you been up to?
    DEXTER. I was sawing logs.
    STANLEY (DEXTER). Please! Could you rephrase that!?!
    DEXTER. Sorry. I was catching forty winks.
    STANLEY (DEXTER). That's better. *(To the others.)* What about you?
    ZOWIE. I was snoozing too.
    CORKY. I took a walk in the woods.
    DEXTER. Excellent idea! Want to go for a walk, Stanley? Look at the trees?
    STANLEY (DEXTER). Been there, been that. On second thought, I noticed this cute little maple on the way up from the plane. I'd like to check out her foliage.
    DEXTER. Then by all means, let's "leaf". *(To the others.)* See you later.

(DEXTER crosses to the front door and exits off UR.)

    CORKY. Dexter seemed funnier when I was a kid. I think he needs some new material.
    ZOWIE. So do I. Dexter's been using the same stuff since Stanley was a twig.
    COLLEEN. *(Backing hurriedly in the door DL. She wears an apron over her dress and is carrying a ladle.)* All right … all right … I'm sorry!

(MRS. THORN storms in after her DL.)

MRS. THORN. I do the cooking here! If I need any help, I'll ask for it!
COLLEEN. I'm sorry, but when I saw the vegetable soup simmering on the stove, I couldn't resist a little taste. It simply cried out for a pinch of celery flakes.
MRS. THORN. *(Snatching the ladle from her.)* You come near my food again and the soup won't be the only thing that cries out! I'm warning you — stay out of my kitchen!

(She takes COLLEEN by the shoulders, turns her around, grabs one sash of the apron, pulls the apron loose from COLLEEN, causing her to jump, then storms out DL.)

CORKY. Hi, Colleen. Been making new friends?
COLLEEN. *(Crossing below the sofa.)* My goodness, that Mrs. Thorn is so temperamental.
ZOWIE. I think she's "mental," period.
COLLEEN. I could give her lots of little cooking tips if she'd let me. After all, I am an expert.
ZOWIE. You could try, but I get the feeling if you touch anything else in there, she might give you a manicure with a meat cleaver.

(COLLEEN frowns and sits on the sofa as CORA appears behind the window from off UL, crosses to the front door and enters.)

CORA. Hi, neighbors! It's good to see ya!
CORKY. Hi, Cora. It's only been a couple of hours ....
CORA. *(Crossing to the others.)* Oh, I know. That's the line I always use when I make my entrance on stage. It just kinda popped out.
ZOWIE. Been for a stroll?
CORA. Shore have. *(Crossing down to them.)* I ain't smelled air this fresh since the time I accidentally sprayed my hair with air freshener 'stead 'a hair spray. Cans looked 'bout the same. I looked a fright, but I smelled like a patch 'a peonies fer a week.

YOU COULD DIE LAUGHING!

(She sits on the sofa by COLLEEN.)

COLLEEN. Accidents can happen. One time I saw a roach in my kitchen — which I cannot abide! — so I grabbed a can of bug spray and coated him with it. Then I realized I had picked up spray starch by mistake.
CORKY. Did it kill him?
COLLEEN. No, but it froze the little sucker in his tracks!
CORKY. I've used stray starch by mistake, too.
ZOWIE. Instead of?
CORKY. Deodorant.
CORA. My goodness! What happened?
CORKY. *(Holding out an arm.)* I spent the rest of the day looking like a prissy little teapot.

(CORKY puts his other hand at his waist and takes a few steps with this pose. Unnoticed by the others, HELENA enters UL. She stops and watches.)

ZOWIE. My turn. I meant to gargle with Listerine ....
CORKY. But instead you used ...?
ZOWIE. *(Speaking through puckered lips.)* Lemon juice.
HELENA. What in the world are you zanies up to?

(HELENA crosses down to above the sofa.)

CORA. Hi there, Helena. I started telling 'bout the time I sprayed my hair with air freshener ....
ZOWIE. *(Cutting in.)* And the rest of us went on to tell about the times we accidentally used one household product instead of another. I'll bet you've done that too.
HELENA. Heck, yes. I spritzed a frying pan with furniture polish instead of Pam cooking spray. You're looking at the inventor of Johnson's Wax burgers. They tasted terrible, but the pan cleaned itself.

(Everyone laughs until MRS. THORN enters DL, carrying a large

knife; the laughter cuts off as abruptly as if someone had flipped a switch. COLLEEN worriedly slips her hands under her legs.)

MRS. THORN. Thought you'd want to know — a man on the radio just said a storm's coming this way. Bad one. Should hit in a couple of hours.
CORKY. Thanks for the info. *(MRS. THORN nods and turns to exit. Under his breath to ZOWIE.)* She'd be perfect as the weather girl for the sci-fi channel.
CORA. Miz Thorn, are there any candles in case the lights go out? You know, from lightning?
MRS. THORN. *(Turning back.)* Since there are no electrical lines from the mainland, the electricity here is provided by a generator. There's enough gasoline to provide power for the weekend, so the lights should be fine. To answer your question, though, there are flashlights and candles in your rooms in case of an unforeseen emergency.
CORA. Oh. Okay.

(MRS. THORN nods again, turns and exits DL.)

ZOWIE. That woman has all the warmth of an ice cube.
HELENA. You're right. If she wanted a cold drink, all she'd have to do is stick her finger in a glass of water.
JOEY. *(Entering UC from off UR.)* I have just been communing with nature. We came to an agreement. I'll stay out of its way if it'll stay out of mine.

(ALLEN and SUSAN enter UL. He seems groggy.)

SUSAN. Are you sure you didn't lay it down somewhere?
ALLEN. I'm positive. I remember dropping it into my flight bag the way I always do.
CORKY. Lose something, Allen?
ALLEN. My key ....
COLLEEN. House key?

YOU COULD DIE LAUGHING! 23

HELENA. Car key?
ALLEN. No, the ignition key to the jet.
CORA. You start a jet plane with a key? I didn't know that.
JOEY. What did you think they do — push it down the runway while the pilot pops the clutch?
CORA. Well, I never thought about it. Actually, there are lots of things I never think about, like, how can they get a whole movie on one 'a them little bitty disk thing-a-ma-bobs?
ZOWIE. Maybe they use little bitty actors.
SUSAN. Can we get back on the subject? We have to find that key; otherwise, we'll be stranded here.
JOEY. Perish the thought.
ALLEN. And I won't be able to fly M. St. Yves over to see you audition.

(This comment energizes the others. CORA and COLLEEN rise. The comics ad-lib comments like "What are we waiting for?," "The key ... we gotta find the key!," etc.)

CORKY. Come on, Zowie — let's search the path. Some of the others have gone for a walk. We'll get them to help us.
HELENA. I'll go with you.
JOEY. Count me in. Being stuck here is not my idea of a good time.

(JOEY, CORKY, ZOWIE and HELENA cross to the front door and exit, crossing out of sight off UR.)

CORA. I'll git the ones who are still in their bedrooms to join in.

(CORA crosses to UL and exits.)

COLLEEN. What can I do?
ALLEN. I'd appreciate it if you'd get Mrs. Thorn to make me a cup of coffee. My head feels woozy. I can't seem to wake up.
COLLEEN. Mrs. Thorn ...? Well .... *(She crosses to the door DL,*

stops and mutters to herself.) I feel like Gretel dropping by the witch's kitchen.

(COLLEEN exits. ALLEN crosses groggily to the table SR and sits on its SL chair.)

SUSAN. Allen, are you okay?

(SUSAN sits on the US chair at the table.)

ALLEN. Not really. Right after we ate lunch, I went to my room to unpack. I had barely got in the door when I started feeling dizzy. I laid down on the bed and passed out cold. I've been out like a light for ... *(He looks at his watch.)* ... five hours.
SUSAN. You must have needed a nap.
ALLEN. I never take naps, besides I still don't feel right. I feel like ... well ... like I've been drugged.
SUSAN. Drugged!?! What on earth ...?
ALLEN. I drank the lemonade Mrs. Thorn made for lunch, like everyone else. If someone put ground-up sleeping pills, for instance, in my glass, the lemon flavor would have masked the tart taste of the drug.
SUSAN. Do you have any idea why someone would do such a thing?
ALLEN. Yes — to steal the key. We can search the island from one end to the other, but I don't think we're going to find it.
SUSAN. Why not?
ALLEN. I remember after I dropped it into my flight bag, I zipped the bag shut. It was still closed, sitting at the foot of the bed, when I zonked out. When I woke up, the bag was still there, but someone had unzipped it.
SUSAN. What reason would anyone have for stealing the ignition key? It doesn't make sense.
ALLEN. We're here with a bunch of comics. Maybe it's one of them's idea of a joke.
SUSAN. Taking the key? That's one thing, but slipping you a

drug to knock you out? That's not a joke — that's dangerous!

ALLEN. Yeah, especially since pilots have to be drug-free before we're allowed to fly. I think the thief intends to keep us all on the island for some reason. Whatever that reason is, it can't be good.

SUSAN. Allen, you're scaring me. What can we do?

ALLEN. For the time being, act like we don't suspect anything is wrong ... that I simply lost the key. I don't want the joker who did this to suspect we're onto him ... or her. If we don't do or say anything to make them put their guard up, maybe they'll slip and give themselves away.

SUSAN. Good idea. And in the meantime, we'll keep our eyes and ears open in case they do.

ALLEN. You got it.

(COLLEEN opens the door DL. She is holding a mug of coffee.)

COLLEEN. Do you want anything in your coffee?

(ALLEN and SUSAN exchange suspicious looks.)

ALLEN. No, just black, thanks.

(COLLEEN enters and crosses to them.)

COLLEEN. *(Handing ALLEN the mug.)* Here you go. Freshly brewed.

ALLEN. Thank you. I hope I didn't put Mrs. Thorn to any trouble.

(He'll sip his coffee.)

COLLEEN. Not at all — Mrs. Thorn wasn't there but Mr. Coffee was, so I made a pot. Susan, dear, I didn't think to ask if you'd like some?

SUSAN. No, thank you, Colleen. *(Rising.)* Colleen, I just remembered .... *(She crosses to above the sofa.)* At lunch I saw you take a small plastic container from your pocket and sprinkle a white powder inside it into a glass of lemonade. *(Turning back to face her.)* What was it?

COLLEEN. *(ALLEN watches her intensely.)* You noticed that? I hope Mrs. Thorn didn't. It was Equal, dear. I always carry some with me — got to watch the waistline, you know; the camera adds ten pounds. I thought the lemonade was a little sour, so I sweetened mine a bit. I didn't want Mrs. Thorn to think I was being critical of her meal, so I slipped it in. Why do you ask?

SUSAN. Oh ... um ... I thought it might have been one of your famous cooking hints you'd share with me.

COLLEEN. Not this time — just plain old artificial sweetener. If you need some later, just ask.

SUSAN. Thanks.

(CORA enters UL followed by ANTONIO, LUCINDA, SAMMY and PAULETTE. They cross down to the others.)

CORA. Hi, neighbors! It's good ta see ya! I rounded up everybody who's still in the house.

LUCINDA. I'll have you know she disturbed my beauty sleep — I need about sixteen hours a day — but that's okay.

ANTONIO. So, like, what's this about a missing key?

ALLEN. I seem to have misplaced the ignition key to the airplane.

ANTONIO. Bummer, but, hey man — if worst comes to worst, I can hot-wire it for you. *(The others give him a look.)* Hey! I grew up in a tough neighborhood!

ALLEN. I appreciate the offer, Antonio, but I don't think it would be a good idea to hot-wire a multi-million-dollar Lear jet.

ANTONIO. Whatever.

SAMMY. In that case, we definitely need to find that key. We'll help you look.

PAULETTE. Yes. I'll go search our room.

SAMMY. *(Stopping her.)* Paulette, Allen hasn't been in our room.

PAULETTE. I know, but when I lose something, it always seems to turn up in the last place I'd think to look for it. *(To the others.)* I lost Sammy once for three days and he turned up in Albuquerque.

SAMMY. *(To the others; sheepishly.)* It's a long story ....

LUCINDA. When I lost a husband, I just went out and found another one. My last spouse said he was from Boulder, Colorado, which makes sense 'cause I think he crawled out from under a rock. I gave him the ax.

PAULETTE. You murdered your husband!?!

LUCINDA. Not really, Paulette — that's just an expression. It means I got rid of him. We divorced.

PAULETTE. I'm so glad you didn't kill him.

LUCINDA. So is he. *(Quietly, to SAMMY.)* I guess you have to watch what you say around Paulette.

SAMMY. You have no idea.

ANTONIO. Do you think you'll ever get hitched again, Lucinda?

LUCINDA. Not unless they drag me down the aisle kicking and screaming. That's an ugly sight; I know — that's how I got number three to the altar, the little twerp. He started wedlock in a headlock. I had a feeling it wouldn't last, though — I bought a wash-and-wear wedding dress for that one.

PAULETTE. Where do you get those?

COLLEEN. That was a joke, Paulette. They don't make polyester and cotton bridal gowns.

PAULETTE. Oh.

SAMMY. You needn't worry about it, Paulette — you're stuck with me till death do us part. You're not just my wife — you're my career.

PAULETTE. Flatterer.

ANTONIO. Hey, no one likes making with the jokes more than I do, but shouldn't we save 'em till the main man is here to hear 'em?

CORA. Antonio's rite — and M. *(She pronounces it "mon-sewer.")* St. Yves kain't git here to hear 'em 'less we find Allen's missing key. We were all in the kitchen and dining room. I'll check those.

(CORA crosses to DL and exits.)

COLLEEN. I'll examine the stairs to the bedrooms in case you dropped it there and it slipped under the carpet runner.... *(She crosses to UL, muttering to herself.)* ... and I'll see how well Mrs. Thorn REALLY cleans.

(COLLEEN exits UL.)

ANTONIO. Me, I'll take a look-see outside. One good thing about wandering in the woods — you don't have to worry about muggers.

(ANTONIO crosses to the front door.)

LUCINDA. *(Following him.)* I'll go with you. I was a Girl Scout so I know what to do if we get lost.
ANTONIO. Really? What's that?
LUCINDA. Scream our heads off.

(ANTONIO and LUCINDA exit and go off UR.)

SUSAN. How do you feel now, Allen?
ALLEN. Better, thanks.
PAULETTE. Oh, dear ... are you ill?
ALLEN. No, Miss Pepper, I ... uh ... I took a nap, which I'm not used to, and was feeling groggy. *(To SUSAN.)* The coffee helped.
PAULETTE. Maybe you should take vitamins. I make Sammy take lots of vitamins every day.
SAMMY. I'll say — A through Zinc, plus other minerals and herbs and who-knows-what? Paulette read that phosphorous was good for your bones and fed me so much of it that I didn't dare scratch my noggin for fear it would blaze up like a match head. I figure after I die, my body will keep going strong for at least a year.
PAULETTE. Don't talk about dying, Sammy, dear. It's bad luck.
SAMMY. Whatever you say, sweet pea.
SUSAN. So you know all about herbs, Paulette.... Sometimes I have a little trouble getting to sleep. Could you recommend anything

YOU COULD DIE LAUGHING!

that would help me?

(SUSAN and ALLEN exchange a glance.)

PAULETTE. Oh, sure. I'll make you a list of herbs you can combine that will knock you out cold.

(SUSAN and ALLEN exchange a knowing look.)

SAMMY. Why don't you do that later? For now, we need to ....

(SAMMY's voice trails off as MR. THORN enters DL.)

MR. THORN. Wife fetched me — said a storm's coming. Heard it on the radio. *(To ALLEN.)* Got some cable loaded on the truck. Should strap down that airplane. Wouldn't want it to blow over.
ALLEN. *(Rising.)* That's a good idea. We can get some of the other men to help us.
SAMMY. Count me in.
PAULETTE. *(Holding up one finger.)* One ....
ALLEN. Corky, Joey and Antonio are outside. We can grab them on the way.
PAULETTE. *(Extending three more fingers.)* Two ... three ... four ....
MR. THORN. Truck's out back.

(MR. THORN starts DL. ALLEN and SAMMY follow.)

SUSAN. *(A whisper to ALLEN as he passes her.)* Be careful. *(He nods, then he and SAMMY follow MR. THORN out DL, exiting. To PAULETTE.)* It is clouding up.
PAULETTE. Oh, dear, I hate storms. They're so ... wet. I left the window up in our room. I'd better close it.
SUSAN. Good thinking.
PAULETTE. Why, thank you, dear. No one ever says that to me.

(She crosses UL and exits. Outside, we hear the sound of the truck engine start. The motor will fade in the distance. SUSAN looks around the room and notices Allen's cup on the table SR. She picks it up and starts toward the door DL. Just before she reaches it, CORA bursts through the door DL, startling SUSAN.)

CORA. *(Entering.)* Hi, neighbor! It's good ta see ya!

SUSAN. It would be good to see you, too, Cora ... if you hadn't startled me half to death.

CORA. Sorry 'bout that. Miz Thorn's back in the kitchen. She shooed me out. She sed she'd keep an eye peeled fer Allen's key. She wuz holdin' a potater peeler when she sed it, so it came out kinda funny, but I didn't dare laugh. I git the feelin' Miz Thorn ain't got no sense 'a humor.

SUSAN. I agree. I'll just give her Allen's coffee cup, then get out of there.

CORA. *(Crossing past SUSAN a few steps SR, then turning back to her.)* Picking up after a man.... Some people mite see that as a sign you're kinda sweet on him.

SUSAN. Allen? No, Cora, we barely know each other. He's been M. St. Yves' private pilot for three years. I got hired just six months ago.

CORA. Really? What did you do before then?

SUSAN. I was a hostess for American Airlines. M. St. Yves needed a larger plane to take his entire staff to Europe on business, so he chartered one of our 747's. I waited on him and he offered me a job as his personal flight attendant. He pays me double what I made before, and I rarely work. I even got to keep my apartment in New York — M. St. Yves sends his plane for me when he needs me. I just have to be on call twenty-four hours a day.

CORA. That's nice. I'm real happy fer ya, Susan.

SUSAN. Thanks.

CORA. I mite 'a been wrong 'bout you and Allen, but if'n ya don't have a steady fella, seems ta me he'd make a mighty good prospect.

SUSAN. Allen is a nice guy, Cora, but I ... uh ... I spend most of

my free time watching out for my dad.
CORA. Is he sick?
SUSAN. He ... he hasn't ... known me ... for years ....
CORA. I'm real sorry ta hear that.
SUSAN. I can always hope things will change. Well ... *(Indicating the cup.)* I'll drop this off in the kitchen, then scurry up the back stairs to my room. I need to unpack my toiletries.

(SUSAN exits DL as COLLEEN enters UL.)

CORA. *(To herself.)* Sweet girl.
COLLEEN. Yes, lovely lady?
CORA. Hi, Colleen. I wuz talkin' 'bout Susan.
COLLEEN. Oh. *(Crossing down to her, DC.)* Yes, I suppose she is. Why were you thinking about her.
CORA. We wuz just chattin'. I told her I thought Allen and her wud make a real fine match.
COLLEEN. You could be right — a pilot and an airline attendant.... You could put a little toy airplane on top of their wedding cake, and the groom could have a sheet cake decorated like a miniature airport runway. Wouldn't that be just darling?
CORA. It shore wud be diff'ernt.
COLLEEN. I'm always full of ideas, and wedding decorations are my specialty.
CORA. Well, if'n I ever git hitched, you'll be the first one I call.

(CORA sits on the sofa.)

COLLEEN. You've never been married?
CORA. Nope. Always figgered I would, but my career always seemed ta keep me too busy ta settle down. How 'bout you?
COLLEEN. I, too, am a bachelor girl. I was engaged once. I ... I haven't told this to many people, but my fiancé, Wally — Wally, the worm — left me at the altar.
CORA. No!
COLLEEN. I'm afraid it's true. There I was in my gorgeous

gown — white silk with a pearl-encrusted, scoop neckline and a ten foot train of Florentine lace, holding a beautiful bouquet of lilies, sprinkled with baby's breath, standing in front of my family and his, our friends, and hundreds of guests. When the preacher said, "Do you, Wallace, take Colleen ...", I reached over and straightened his boutonniere, a white rosebud, and Wally suddenly screamed out, "That's it! I can't stand it anymore! You're perfect, Colleen. I'm not and never will be, but you'd spend the next fifty years trying to make me an ideal husband! You don't need a man, Colleen, you need a mannequin! ... one you can adjust and pick at and dress in color-coordinated clothes with perfectly matched pocket handkerchiefs and ties! Maybe you can find the mate you need in a department store window! As for me, I'm outta here!"... and thirty seconds later, he was.

CORA. That's awful!

COLLEEN. It was the most embarrassing moment of my life.

CORA. I 'spect so! That had ta hurt worse than stubbin' a toe on the bed post!

COLLEEN. Yes, it was painful. *(She sits on the sofa beside CORA.)* Perhaps Wally was right. Perhaps I should elope with Dexter's little wooden friend, Stanley, and forget about real men altogether.

CORA. *(Putting an arm around COLLEEN's shoulder.)* Now, now, gal .... The rite man fer you is out there somewhere. I always believed there's a perfect man fer every woman. My mama used to say, "There's a bee fer ev'ry flower. Your bee will find you if'n ya don't act like a bloomin' idiot". Yore bee will come along someday, honey. You wait an' see if'n it don't.

COLLEEN. Thanks, Cora. I hope your bee finds you, too.

(CORA AND COLLEEN hug.)

DEXTER. *(Entering UC with STANLEY.)* Hello, again, ladies. It's clouding over and the wind is beginning to pick up out there.

COLLEEN. There's a storm approaching. Mrs. Thorn heard it on the radio.

DEXTER. In that case, I had better keep Stanley inside. He does-

n't like to get wet.
 STANLEY (DEXTER). You wouldn't either if getting water-logged made mushrooms sprout on your bottom.
 DEXTER. I suppose not. *(To the others.)* Where is everybody?
 COLLEEN. The other men have gone with Mr. Thorn to lash down the plane.
 DEXTER. That explains it.... Stanley and I heard a truck go by down the path. We had gone exploring in the woods. Stanley is into genealogy.
 COLLEEN. He is?
 STANLEY (DEXTER). Yeah — I was looking up my ancestors.
 CORA. The rest of us have been searchin' fer Allen's key to the plane. 'Parently he misplaced it.
 COLLEEN. And he can't start the engine without it.
 DEXTER. Oh, dear.... It would be a shame if M. St. Yves couldn't get here to see us audition.
 CORA. *(Rising.)* Shoot! I'm gonna try out fer 'im if'n I haft-a swim back to the mainland to do it!
 DEXTER. That's a pretty far distance, and, besides, I believe there are sharks in those waters.
 STANLEY (DEXTER). *(Humming the first couple of bars of the theme music from the movie "Jaws."*)* Dum-dum, dum-dum, dum-dum, dum-dum ....
 COLLEEN. Then I, for one, will stay put. Fish is one of my favorite dishes; I don't want one saying the same thing about me. *(She eyes DEXTER, getting an idea. Rising.)* Uh ... Dexter ... if we should become stranded here, I have no one at home to miss me but my cat. Do you ... uh ... have a Mrs. Porter at home to worry about you?

(COLLEEN will inch over to him.)

 DEXTER. My mother is no longer with us.
 COLLEEN. *(Inching closer.)* I mean, do you have a wife?
 DEXTER. I did a long time ago, but not anymore.

---

*Permission to use the *Theme from Jaws* must be obtained from Universal Pictures, 825 8th Avenue, 30th Floor, New York, NY 10019.

COLLEEN. Really? *(She inches right next to him.)* How interesting ... the two of us ... single and unencumbered ....
CORA. *(Rising.)* Hey! I'm uncucumbered, too!

(CORA will move till she's on the other side of DEXTER.)

COLLEEN. Alone in the world ....
CORA. No one to talk to ....
DEXTER. But I'm not alone, dear ladies. I have a child.
COLLEEN. You do?
STANLEY (DEXTER). Sure he does! He's got me!
CORA. But ....
DEXTER. *(Cutting in.)* Stanley's right — I have him, and as long as he's around, I'll always have somebody to talk to.
CORA. You talk to Stanley when yore by yoreselves?
DEXTER. Naturally.
CORA. *(Under her breath to COLLEEN.)* He's all yores. *(Out loud to DEXTER as she starts DL.)* Well, it's been nice chattin' with you ... both of you ... but I think I'll pop out back fer a breath of air afore the storm gits here.
COLLEEN. *(Edging DL.)* I'll go breathe whatever oxygen you aren't using. *(To DEXTER.)* I'm sure I'll ... uh ... see you at dinner if not before.

(Following CORA, they EXIT DL.)

STANLEY (DEXTER). They're acting a bit odd, don't you think?
DEXTER. You took the words right out of my mouth.

(There is a rumble of thunder. ZOWIE, LUCINDA and HELENA rush in UC from off UR. They will pause and catch their breath. DEXTER will cross up to them.)

HELENA. Made it! ... and judging by that thunder, not a moment too soon!

LUCINDA. I haven't moved that fast since I chased husband number four around the boudoir on our wedding night! He was a quick little dude ....

HELENA. Did you catch him?

LUCINDA. Finally, but by that time I was too pooped to care.

ZOWIE. Lucinda, honey, I hate to tell you, but I think it's the men who usually chase the women.

LUCINDA. Zowie, honey, if I'd waited for that to happen, I never would have got married.

(LUCINDA plops down onto the window seat. The sky outside the window behind her will continue to grow very dark.)

ZOWIE. Let's get a man's opinion. Dexter, what do you think? Do you like forward women?

DEXTER. Funny you should ask that ....

STANLEY (DEXTER). We don't have time for romance. We have our career to think about.

ZOWIE. Yeah, well, who doesn't? ... but there's more to life than being a star.

STANLEY (DEXTER). For you, maybe, but without the spotlight, I'm nothing.

HELENA. We see your point, Stanley, but, Dexter, you're a living, human being with emotions ....

STANLEY (DEXTER). Hey! Hold it! You think just because I'm made of wood I don't have feelings!?!

HELENA. Well ....

STANLEY (DEXTER). I know when I've been insulted! Let's go, Dexter.

DEXTER. As you wish, Stanley. *(Coolly.)* Excuse us, ladies.

(He crosses to UR and EXITS as the others watch him with "I don't believe this" expressions.)

ZOWIE. Can you believe that?

LUCINDA. Who does that little knothole think he is, Pinocchio?

HELENA. I've always suspected ventriloquists were a little weird.
ZOWIE. A "little" weird!?! That's like saying King Kong was "slightly annoyed" by those pesky airplanes.
LUCINDA. I agree with you, girls. I've dated a lot of show business types, but never a ventriloquist. I did go out with a sword swallower, though: "The Great Gilbert."
HELENA. What happened?
LUCINDA. It didn't last long. I told a joke just as Gilbert was swallowing a sword. He doubled over laughing. It was ghastly.
HELENA. You don't mean ...?
LUCINDA. It didn't kill him, but in one fell swoop, he gave himself a tonsillectomy, appendectomy, and snipped off his gall bladder. He never asked me out again.
ZOWIE. You're joking, right? Tell me that was a joke.
LUCINDA. If I'm lying, may I be struck dead on the spot. *(There is another crash of thunder, closer this time. LUCINDA jumps up.)* It's a lie! ... a BIG lie! ... Sooooo biggggg ...

(SUSAN and PAULETTE enter UL. Both carry cell phones.)

PAULETTE. I didn't remove it. If I had, I'm sure I would remember ... well ... pretty sure ....
SUSAN. I don't think you did, Paulette. I think whoever took yours took mine as well.
HELENA. Took what? What's going on?
PAULETTE. I just tried to use our cell phone to call our answering service. It wouldn't work. I opened the thing-a-ma-gig to check the battery and it's gone. I heard Susan in her room next door and asked her if she has a cell phone.
SUSAN. *(Holding hers up.)* I do, but its battery has been taken out as well.
LUCINDA. As husband number one said as we walked down the aisle, "I don't like where this is going."
ZOWIE. I called my agent on my phone before I laid down to take a nap. I put it in my pocket after I woke up and have had it on me ever since. *(She takes a cell phone from her pocket and pushes a but-*

YOU COULD DIE LAUGHING! 37

ton on it, then pushes it several times.) Nothing. *(She opens a compartment and looks inside.)* No battery. Someone took it while I was asleep.

    SUSAN. We can check the phones of the others who have them, but I feel sure the results are going to be the same.

    PAULETTE. I don't understand what's happening ....

    HELENA. For once, Paulette, you're not the only one. First Allen's key goes missing, and now this. Why?

    SUSAN. Isn't it obvious? Someone intended to isolate us here on this island ... and they have.

(Thunder. The lights fade to blackout.
A stagehand sets the clock hands to 7:45.)

Scene 3

(Friday night. About 8:00 p.m.
The room lights fade up. The storm has hit and is raging outside. There is the sound of rain pouring down and intermittent flashes of lightning followed by thunder. A fire [electric logs] is burning in the fireplace. On stage are SAMMY and PAULETTE on the window seat; DEXTER with STANLEY and HELENA on the fireplace bench; CORKY, ZOWIE, CORA and ANTONIO at the table; SUSAN, ALLEN, COLLEEN on the sofa; and JOEY and LUCINDA on the chairs below the sofa. All look dejected.)

    PAULETTE. *(After a beat.)* It's raining outside.

(The others turn their heads in unison to give PAULETTE a look, then — again in unison — turn back.)

    SAMMY. A very astute observation, my dear.

    PAULETTE. Thank you. I'm not quite sure what "astute" means, but it sounds like a compliment, so thank you.

SAMMY. You're welcome.
HELENA. I'm chilly. Could someone throw another log on the fire?
STANLEY (DEXTER). Don't look at me!
ANTONIO. *(Rising.)* I got-cha covered.

(ANTONIO will cross to the fireplace and put a log from the hearth into it.)

ZOWIE. I gotta tell you, this is the pits! Here we got a room full of the funniest comedians on the planet, and it's like we're at a wake, or something. If one of you guys is playing a practical joke, you've taken it far enough. 'Fess up and we'll let bygones be bygones. *(No one responds.)* Aw, come on.... Corky, is it you?
CORKY. Me? No way! I was betting on Antonio. It wouldn't be the first time he pulled something like this.
ANTONIO. Say what!?! I'm sorry I ever told you 'bout that, man! Just because I spent a little time in the slammer when I was a kid does not make me the guilty party!
HELENA. You've been behind bars, Antonio?
JOEY. Why does that not surprise me?
HELENA. Was it for stealing?
ANTONIO. I didn't "steal" nothing — I just borrowed it. See, some of my buddies and me needed this guy's car to go for a little ride ... we just forgot to tell the dude we were taking it, that's all.
CORA. Where were you goin'?
ANTONIO. Just a little ways.
HELENA. How little?
ANTONIO. From Brooklyn, New York, to Orlando, Florida. We wanted to see Disney World. Hey, I told you we were just kids.
PAULETTE. Sammy and I went to Disney World once. I loved it — seeing all the cartoon characters walking around. My favorite character is Goofy.
SAMMY. *(Patting her hand.)* My favorite character is "goofy," too.
ANTONIO. Wouldn't know 'bout that. We only got as far as Macon, Georgia. When the guy discovered his Chevy was missing, he

reported it to the cops, and they put out an APB on it. We got picked up by some hick sheriff who tossed us in the hoosegow.

CORA. I've entertained at prisons before. There are some real creepy criminals in thar.

(CORA takes a few mints from the bowl and lays them on the table. During the scene, she will push them around with a finger, one at a time, unconsciously, making patterns with them. She doesn't eat any.)

ANTONIO. Tell me 'bout it, Cora! My cellmates would have been right at home at a convention of Missing Links. I was so scared my knees were shaking like a hula dancer in a hurricane! As terrifying as it was, though, that's where my career as a stand-up comic began.

ALLEN. In a jail cell in Georgia?

ANTONIO. Yep. I've always had a smart mouth on me ... *(Moving about at will.)* ... and whenever I get nervous, I tend to talk like a parrot on uppers. Well, that day the smart-alec remarks came flying out of me -- and those goons started laughing. The more I talked, the more they laughed. I figure it saved my skin — I mean, you're not gonna beat up on somebody that makes you laugh, right? *(He goes into a comic routine, "playing the room.")* "Hey, big fella, is that your head or are you carrying a boulder on your shoulder? I'm Antonio, what's your name? Jimmy Lee? Nice teeth, Jimmy Lee — all five of 'em! I like your tattoos.... By the way, "death" has an "a" in it! "Mom" is spelled right, though. Homemade, huh? You really made those with a switchblade and a bottle of ink? And they say good penmanship is going out of style. You did your own piercings, too, huh? How 'bout that! It must be nice to know if you ever rip your pants, you have some safety pins handy. Who are you? Buford? I wish I had hair like that, Buford ... but on my head instead 'a my back. If you ever run short 'a cash, you can shave it, weave it, and sell it as doormats." *(Dropping the routine.)* You get the idea. By the time my mama wired the bail money, my fellow felons and I were the best of friends ... and I had found my calling. Incidentally, that experience taught me a lesson — that and my mama's fly swatter on my backside — and I never took anything ever again. That includes Allen's missing key and the cell phone batteries. If I'm lyin', I'm dyin'!

(ANTONIO sits back at the table.)

    LUCINDA. I believe you, Antonio.
    HELENA. So do I, but somebody took those items. We've searched the lodge from top to bottom; maybe we should do the same to each other.
    SUSAN. You mean conduct a strip search? Really, Helena, no one here would be dumb enough to hide those things on their person ....

(SUSAN pauses a beat, realizing there might be one. In unison, she and the others turn their heads to look at PAULETTE who sits there with an innocent smile on her face. In unison, the others turn back.)

    ALLEN. I doubt if a body search would do any good.
    HELENA. Probably not, but I have some expensive new undies I was dying to show off. Just forget it.
    JOEY. Searching is a waste of time. The thief could just as easily have buried the key and batteries somewhere in the woods where we'd never find them.
    COLLEEN. That's true. You know, the culprit isn't necessarily one of us. There are two other people in this house who could have taken the missing items.
    CORKY. You mean the Thorns? ... or as I've come to think of them, The Munsters Go to Gilligan's Island?
    COLLEEN. Precisely. They're both pretty suspicious characters, if you ask me ... and I'm not just saying that because Mrs. Thorn makes me feel as welcome in her kitchen as a patch of poison ivy at a nudist camp.
    SAMMY. Colleen has a point. Mr. Thorn lives up to his name, too. He's a cantankerous old codger.
    PAULETTE. I've always wondered, dear.... What's a codger?

YOU COULD DIE LAUGHING! 41

SAMMY. A codger is a coot with a bad attitude.
PAULETTE. Oh.
ALLEN. No one's going to argue with you that the Thorns could be up to no good, but why? For what purpose? They could get fired for pulling a stunt like this.
STANLEY (DEXTER). Unless they're following orders.
CORA. Whose orders? Oh…. You mean M. St. Yves?
STANLEY (DEXTER). He pulls their strings … a process I'm familiar with.
CORA. But why would M. St. Yves have the Thorns strand us here?
ALLEN. It would be for a purpose. He's not the type to pull practical jokes.
SUSAN. I agree. Everything with M. St. Yves is strictly business.
ANTONIO. Maybe it's like, you know, a test.
CORA. Oh, I hope not. I never wuz good at quizzes.
CORKY. I see where Antonio's coming from. Maybe the big man is testing our resourcefulness … our inventiveness … our ability to function during a crisis!
ANTONIO. Right on!

(CORKY and ANTONIO give each other a high five.)

ZOWIE. If that's true, then this is a process of elimination. M. St. Yves can use only one us on this show he's planning. We all know there's a lot of pressure making a TV show. This could be his way of finding out who among us has still got what it takes.
LUCINDA. A process of elimination … the same method I used to pick my husbands. I hope he's better at it than I was.
CORA. I, fer one, ain't the kind ta beat around the bush. If y'all think the Thorns are pullin' these pranks, let's git 'em in here an' ask 'em.
CORKY. Yeah! Let's grab them and grill them like a couple of weenies on the Fourth of July!

(Some of the others murmur agreement.)

COLLEEN. If you can find them.
HELENA. What?
COLLEEN. A few minutes ago I went into the kitchen to ask Mrs. Thorn if I might have a cup of herbal tea ... preferably Earl Gray chamomile, naturally decaffeinated, if she had any. I find a cup of tea to be the perfect beverage to sip on a wet, stormy night, don't you?
HELENA. Get to the point, Colleen.
COLLEEN. Well, Mrs. Thorn wasn't in the kitchen or dining area. When I knocked on the door to the servants' quarters at the back of the lodge, no one answered. I don't know where she and Mr. Thorn are.
HELENA. Has anyone seen them?
STANLEY (DEXTER). I haven't.
ZOWIE. Not since supper, when we all went to our rooms to freshen up.

(The others murmur they haven't either.)

PAULETTE. *(Looking at her watch.)* It's only eight o'clock. Surely they haven't gone to bed. Maybe they went outside.
SAMMY. In this storm? Paulette, only a maniac would go out on a night like this.

(MR. THORN appears right behind them outside the window, from off UL. He is wearing a yellow rain slicker with a hood which is pulled over his head. It is dripping wet. He puts the palms of his hands against the glass and peers inside. Everyone, who had turned toward SAMMY and PAULETTE, jumps and cries out, startled. PAULETTE and SAMMY look behind them. PAULETTE screams. Everyone ad-libs excitedly as MR. THORN crosses to the door US and enters. Everyone but SAMMY and PAULETTE rises. SAMMY holds PAULETTE protectively.)

SUSAN. Mr. Thorn! You gave us a terrible fright!
MR. THORN. *(Crossing to DC.)* Sorry 'bout that.
ZOWIE. What on earth were you doing out there? In that wind,

you could get killed by a falling tree limb!
MR. THORN. Had to go out. Was looking for Mrs. Thorn.
COLLEEN. You, too?
ALLEN. How long has she been missing?
MR. THORN. *(He sits on the chair SL of the table.)* Couple of hours. After supper, after you all went upstairs, she started clearing the table. Told me to check all the windows downstairs — be sure no rain was blowing in. I did. When I went back to the kitchen, she was gone. T'wasn't no where to be found.

(MR. THORN absently picks up the mints CORA put on the table.)

ANTONIO. So you, like, looked outside?
MR. THORN. *(He pops the mints into his mouth and chews them during his dialog.)* Yeah. When we stay here, Mrs. Thorn always throws the table scraps out back; the raccoons and other critters eat 'em. I thought she might have stepped out and ... I dunno ... maybe the door blew shut or something.... So I put on my rain slicker and went to find her. Looked all over this side 'a the island. No sign 'a the missus.
ANTONIO. We'll help you, man! Got any more of those raincoats?
MR. THORN. There's a supply in the coat closet.

(MR. THORN indicates UR.)

SAMMY. *(Rising; to PAULETTE.)* Stay here, Paulette.

(SAMMY and the other men, except DEXTER, cross to the closet UR, take out rain slickers like the one MR. THORN is wearing and put them on. DEXTER carries STANLEY to UL.)

DEXTER. I'll join you shortly after I put Stanley to bed.
STANLEY (DEXTER). Thank goodness! I've been terrified of storms ever since my uncle ELM-er was struck by lightning. It split him right down the middle!

(DEXTER exits UL.)

JOEY. After he's hired me, I must ask M. St. Yves how Dexter made his list of possibilities.

SAMMY. Counting chickens, are you, Joey?

PAULETTE. Chickens? I don't see any chickens. I haven't seen a chicken since the last time I ate one.

CORKY. If we can get back to the problem at hand.... Ladies, you can search the lodge from top to bottom while we men check outside ... if that's not too chauvinistic a suggestion.

COLLEEN. Heck, no. I prefer it that way. If I get my hair wet, I can't do a thing with it.

CORA. Poor Mrs. Thorn.... If she's got hurt, how'll we ever git help here for her?

SAMMY. We can cross that bridge when we come to it.

LUCINDA. I wish there were a bridge — right over to the mainland. I'd be the first one on it. I haven't been this nervous since my first appearance on David Letterman's *(or name any talk show host)* show and I accidentally turned over a pitcher of ice water onto his lap.

HELENA. How embarrassing! What did he say?

LUCINDA. I don't remember, but his voice was two octaves higher.

ALLEN. We're ready when you are, Mr. Thorn.

(MR. THORN rises slowly. A strange expression comes to his face. He starts to gasp, then grabs his throat. He staggers, gasping, then falls to the floor DC. COLLEEN screams. Everyone reacts, startled. PAULETTE rises; SAMMY rushes to her. HELENA, LUCINDA and COLLEEN cluster DL in a frightened huddle. ANTONIO rushes to ZOWIE as CORKY rushes to CORA; both couples huddle DR. SUSAN and ALLEN rush to MR. THORN and kneel beside him.)

SUSAN. I've had CPR. *(She feels his wrist for a pulse.)* He's dead.

YOU COULD DIE LAUGHING! 45

(The others ad-lib shocked reactions.)

CORA. He wuz ... he wuz worried 'bout his wife.... Wuz it his heart? A heart attack?
ANTONIO. Uh-uh! Didn't look like no heart attack to me — not grabbing his throat and all. Looked to me like he might'a been poisoned.
CORA. Poisoned?!?

(Everyone ad-libs, upset.)

ZOWIE. He just ate some of those mints you had been playing with, Cora, right before he keeled over. During a hiatus when my show was on, I did a guest shot in a TV movie — a murder mystery. The victim on it got poisoned. Allen, smell his lips. *(Puzzled, ALLEN leans over MR. THORN's body and smells near his mouth.)* Garlic?
ALLEN. Yes. How did you know?
ZOWIE. Arsenic. That's how the guy on the show got done in — with arsenic. It leaves the scent of garlic around the victim's mouth.
CORA. There was poison on them mints?!? You mean if'n I had et one 'a them ....

(She swoons. CORKY catches her and sits with her on the bench.)

COLLEEN. You think Mr. Thorn was ... murdered?

(ALLEN and SUSAN rise.)

ALLEN. So it appears.

(More ad-libs, concerned.)

COLLEEN. Maybe something happened where the candy was made. Not everyone keeps their kitchen as spotless as mine.
JOEY. That sounds like a possibility.
CORKY. It didn't go down that way. The mints were fine this

afternoon — I ate one ... whole.
 PAULETTE. Sammy, I don't feel so well ....
 SAMMY. You need to lie down. *(To the others.)* I'm going to take Paulette to our room.

(SAMMY leads her a couple of steps SL; when they clear the window seat, we see a piece of cloth, which had been hidden by PAULETTE's skirt when she was seated, sticking out from under the lid of the window seat.)

 ALLEN. Wait a minute! *(SAMMY and PAULETTE stop UL.)* What's that?

(ALLEN crosses to the window seat, followed by SUSAN.)

 SUSAN. It's a piece of material caught in the window seat. It looks like ....

(ALLEN raises the lid of the window seat. SUSAN gasps and turns away.)

 ALLEN. We've found Mrs. Thorn. *(SAMMY turns PAULETTE away from the sight.)* There's an electric mixer beside her; its cord is wrapped around her neck. She's been strangled to death.

(The others react, shocked.)

 HELENA. *(Softly.)* Zowie was right — we knew we were brought here for a process of elimination. What we hadn't figured, though, was that someone obviously plans to eliminate us PERMANENTLY!
 COLLEEN. Are you saying somebody intends to kill us?
 JOEY. You picked up on that real quick, Colleen.
 COLLEEN. There's no need to be sarcastic. I picked up on something else, too.

JOEY. What?
COLLEEN. The Thorns are dead. If there's no one else on this island, then that means the murderer has to be one of us.

(Everyone looks at one another suspiciously as the lights fade out.)

CURTAIN

ACT II

Scene 1

(Saturday morning. About 1:00 a.m.
It is several hours later, about 1:00 a.m., though a STAGEHAND has set the clock at 12:30 just before the curtain rises. The storm has passed and dark moonlight wafts in and out beyond the window. The fire has burned out; the room is softly lit by lamp light. The Thorns' bodies have been removed. The women, except SUSAN, are onstage. LUCINDA is seated on the sofa, her feet on the coffee table, sound asleep. CORA sits beside her. PAULETTE is on the window seat, looking out the window. HELENA and ZOWIE stand above the table SR. ZOWIE holds a large ziplock bag open while HELENA, wearing rubber kitchen gloves, is putting the mint dish and mints into the bag. The mint dish from the coffee table and its mints are in a bag, also on the table. COLLEEN paces CS from left to right and back, nervously.)

PAULETTE. I wish Sammy were here.

ZOWIE. The men should be back soon, Paulette. It's bound to take them several hours to search the entire island thoroughly.

HELENA. At least the storm has passed. *(She pulls her hands out of the bag.)* There.

ZOWIE. Got it. *(She zips the bag shut. HELENA will remove the gloves and lay them on the table.)* The evidence is all bagged, just like we did it in that TV movie.

COLLEEN. If there are any fingerprints on the mint dishes I didn't see any, and I notice that kind of thing. The murderer probably wiped them clean.

HELENA. No doubt you're right, Colleen, but it doesn't hurt to protect them, just in case.

LUCINDA. *(Talking in her sleep.)* Romeo, Romeo, your Juliet awaits, you sexy thing, you!

(LUCINDA giggles girlishly.)

HELENA. Good grief! If Lucinda talks in her sleep like that every night, no wonder she couldn't keep a husband.

(SUSAN enters DL, carrying a tray with a pot of cocoa and several mugs.)

SUSAN. I made hot cocoa, if anyone wants some.

(She crosses to the table SR.)

ZOWIE. I'd like a cup.

(She puts the bagged mint dishes on the mantle. SUSAN puts the tray on the table, then pours a mug of cocoa.)

HELENA. That sounds good.

(HELENA reaches for the mug SUSAN poured, then hesitates.)

SUSAN. I don't blame you, Helena. We should all stay on our guard till the killer is caught.
CORA. If'n he's caught ... or she.
COLLEEN. *(Coming to SR of the sofa.)* You don't think one of us women could kill someone? Especially Mrs. Thorn, strangled with a cord like that? It would be so ... unladylike.
HELENA. Lucretia Borgia was a lady, and she poisoned people left and right.

ZOWIE. And as for violent crimes, well, Lizzie Borden had an ax to grind with her whole family.
COLLEEN. Okay ... okay ... you've made your point.
SUSAN. I can assure you this is just cocoa. See? *(She sips from the mug.)* Help yourselves.

(SUSAN crosses to the fireplace bench and sits. HELENA and ZOWIE pour cocoa for themselves. They will sit on the chairs DL. COLLEEN crosses to the table and pours a cup. She'll sit at the table and sip it.)

LUCINDA. *(Still asleep.)* Stop that, you big hunk-a, hunk-a burning love!

(More giggles.)

CORA. *(Nudging her.)* Wake up, Lucinda, before you make me break out in a sweat. *(LUCINDA mumbles, waking up.)* Susan fixed us some cocoa.
LUCINDA. Huh ... what?... Darn! I was having a terrific dream.
CORA. We know — you talk in your sleep. It sounded like that one should'a been rated PG-13.
LUCINDA. They all start that way, then they progress to RRH.
CORA. RRH? What's that?
LUCINDA. Really, Really Hot!
CORA. Let's have some cocoa. In the state yore in, it'll pro'bly cool you down.

(CORA and LUCINDA rise, cross to the table and pour cocoa.)

SUSAN. Paulette, I'll be glad to pour you a mug.
PAULETTE. No, thank you, dear.
CORA. I been thinkin'.... Maybe we're worryin' 'bout nothin'. That didn't sound rite — a'course when two people git brutally murdered, yore gonna worry — but whut I mean is, maybe somebody had

a grudge 'a some kind against the Thorns in particular. Maybe whoever killed 'em ain't got no reason to harm the rest of us.

HELENA. I'd like to agree with you, Cora, but that's not the way it is. Mrs. Thorn was clearly a targeted victim, but any of us could have eaten the poisoned mints. You know you came close, yourself, playing with them like you did.

CORA. That's true. In that case, the murderer didn't care who he bumped off.

(CORA and LUCINDA will take their mugs of cocoa back to the sofa and sit.)

ZOWIE. What I can't figure is, what's the killer's motive? When people kill people, it's usually for a reason.

COLLEEN. Unless the murderer is insane ....

ZOWIE. I don't think so — not in this case. It's one thing when a person "snaps" and goes off on a killing spree, but poisoning the mints — that's premeditated. And stranding us here — that was planned, too. This way, the murderer can pick us off, one by one.

LUCINDA. Which brings us back to the motive. Why?

ZOWIE. I think when we know "why" we'll know "who."

(Flashlight beams are seen beyond the window.)

PAULETTE. They're back! The men are back! *(She jumps up. The men enter.)* Sammy! *(SAMMY crosses to PAULETTE, hugs her, puts his flashlight on the window seat, then crosses to the closet UR where the other men are removing and hanging their rain slickers. SAMMY does so too. The men will put their flashlights on the tables or mantle. As this action occurs:)* I was so worried, dear. Did you find anyone?

SAMMY. Not a soul. There's no one on this island except us.

ALLEN. Did anything happen while we were gone?

CORA. Nope. It was quieter'n a tomb ... uh ... fergit I sed that.

COLLEEN. After you put the Thorns in their bedroom and left,

YOU COULD DIE LAUGHING! 53

we stayed together in here, pretty much. After what happened, I certainly have no intention of going off anywhere by myself.
    DEXTER. That's a good idea. I hated to leave Stanley alone in our room. If you'll excuse me, I'll go get him.

(DEXTER exits UL.)

    JOEY. *(Muttering to himself, sarcastically.)* Lucky us ....
    ANTONIO. That Dexter is a trip! Like, what's anybody gonna do to that little blockhead? Whittle him down to a pile of wood shavings?
    SUSAN. I would. If I got a chance, I'd take a hatchet and chop the thing into kindling. *(The others react to this comment.)* Sorry ... I've never liked ventriloquists' dummies.
    ZOWIE. I know what you mean. They give me the creeps. When one opens its mouth, it's like a coat rack started talking to you. It's not natural.
    PAULETTE. Well, I think Stanley's cute.
    ZOWIE. So are Barbie dolls, but I don't want to have a conversation with one.
    HELENA. Susan made some cocoa, if anyone wants some.
    CORKY. Sounds good. I'm cold and wet all over.
    LUCINDA. That's what husband number one said after I pushed him off the Staten Island ferry. *(The others give her a look.)* Hey, he deserved it! He had just told me he was leaving me for another woman. I figured I'd let her have what she deserved — a big drip!
    COLLEEN. *(Rising.)* This cocoa's good. I'm going to have a refill.

(She crosses to the table DR and is joined there by ALLEN, CORKY, SAMMY, JOEY and ANTONIO. All pour themselves cocoa. PAULETTE crosses to the window seat where SAMMY will join her with his. CORKY and ANTONIO will sit at the table as will COLLEEN and JOEY after they pour their cocoa. ALLEN takes SUSAN's arm and will lead her DC. They will hold a quiet conversation while the others are busy with the cocoa.)

ALLEN. While we were out, I searched the plane again.

SUSAN. Did you find anything?

ALLEN. It's what I didn't find.... Remember the gun M. St. Yves had me keep in the cockpit's storage compartment?

SUSAN. In case we ever had to make a forced landing in the wilderness ....

ALLEN. ... and had to protect ourselves from wolves or other wild animals, yes. Well, it's gone.

SUSAN. *(Surprised.)* The gun is missing?

ALLEN. I'm afraid so ... and that's not the only one. Before we — the other men and I — left to search the island, I slipped into the Thorns' room.

SUSAN. The Thorns' ...?

ALLEN. Yes. Remember yesterday when I told all of you I saw Mr. Thorn shoot a snake once?

SUSAN. I remember.

ALLEN. I thought I had better find his gun. Apparently, the killer beat me to it.

SUSAN. What do you mean?

ALLEN. I was looking through the Thorns' things, and when I pulled out their top bureau drawer, I found an open box of bullets, the lid lying beside it, and some of the bullets spilled in the drawer. I think it's safe to assume someone found the gun, loaded it, and took it with them.

SUSAN. *(Frowning.)* So two guns are missing, the one from the plane and Mr. Thorn's ... and the killer could have both of them. Should we search everyone's room?

ALLEN. No. If the killer hid the jet key and phone batteries away from the lodge, he or she probably hid the guns as well, or — worse — if the guns are on them, they could pull them out and start firing if we tried to search them.

SUSAN. Oh, dear ...

ALLEN. Keep your eyes and ears open, and don't tell anyone else. There's no need to start a panic.

SUSAN. I won't breathe a word.

(At this point the others are going to their seats. ALLEN and SUSAN cross to the bench and sit.)

CORA. While y'all wuz lookin' 'round, ya didn't happen ta stumble acrost a boat, did ya? Somethin' that'd git us off this island?

ANTONIO. No such luck, Cora, but I discovered the rat poison that was probably used to kill Mr. Thorn, though. The garage where he kept the truck is used as a tool shed. The box of poison is sitting there on a shelf, out in plain sight.

CORKY. The garage door was open all day. I noticed that when I took a walk this afternoon.

JOEY. Did you notice the rat poison this afternoon?

CORKY. No, and don't start getting any ideas! Everybody was in and out of the lodge today. Any of us could have seen it.

CORKY. It occurred to me that would be a good place to hide the missing key and batteries, so I gave it a quick once-over.

ZOWIE. And?

CORKY. Nothing ... unless you count a bunch of mummified flies caught in some spider webs.

ZOWIE. That's what I feel like right now — a fly caught in a web.

(DEXTER enters UL with STANLEY.)

DEXTER. Stanley's fine.

STANLEY (DEXTER). What did you have to wake me up for? I was dead to the world. *(To the others.)* Hi, folks.

(The others, except JOEY and SUSAN, mutter greetings like "hi" or "hey, Stanley.")

ANTONIO. *(To CORKY.)* Aw, man, tell me I didn't just say "hi" to a piece of lumber.

CORKY. We all did. You gotta admit, the little guy has a personality. That's what a good ventriloquist does — he creates a persona for his dummy that makes the character seem real.

ANTONIO. I guess so, but it still feels weird to talk to a little guy who has a knothole for a navel.

COLLEEN. We're all having cocoa, Dexter. Would you like me to pour you a mug?

DEXTER. No, thank you, Colleen. I'm diabetic — can't have sugar.

STANLEY (DEXTER). I never drink anything — I tend to retain water.

ZOWIE. Hey, Dexter ... Stanley ... keep going.

LUCINDA. Yeah — we could all use a few laughs right now.

(DEXTER will cross to CS where he will do a part of his act. All but SUSAN and JOEY will respond. She watches, but is pensive, uninvolved. The audience might notice this or they might not. JOEY will watch the performers with a smug expression; it's clear he thinks his act is better than theirs.)

DEXTER. Come over here, Stanley. We need to have a little talk.

STANLEY (DEXTER). Whatever you say.

DEXTER. You are in trouble, young man. I just got a call from your principal.

STANLEY (DEXTER). Uh-oh ....

DEXTER. Miss Paddlebottom informed me you're failing three subjects: English, math and science.

STANLEY (DEXTER). Yeah, but I got an A in social studies.

DEXTER. How did you manage that?

STANLEY (DEXTER). The teacher gave everyone whose forefathers came over on the Mayflower an extra ten points. She gave me a hundred when I told her my great-great-great-great-grandfather WAS the Mayflower.

DEXTER. Pretty crafty.

STANLEY (DEXTER). I thought so.

DEXTER. That still doesn't explain why you're flunking your other subjects. What's the problem, Stanley?

STANLEY (DEXTER). I can't concentrate, Dexter. I'm in love.
DEXTER. Ahhh.... The sap is rising.
STANLEY (DEXTER.) No, he's not — Corky's still sitting down.

(CORKY reacts, surprised. The others, except SUSAN and JOEY, laugh.)

DEXTER. What I meant is, you're growing up, Stanley. When you start to notice girls, your childhood is over.
ANTONIO. *(Giving CORKY a friendly punch on the arm.)* Don't worry, Corky — one of these days a girl is going to notice you back.

(Everyone except SUSAN and JOEY laughs.)

CORKY. *(Punching ANTONIO's arm.)* Hey! What is this, get Corky day?
STANLEY (DEXTER). Do you mind? We're working up here!
ANTONIO & CORKY. Sorry.
DEXTER. So, tell me, Stanley, this girl you're infatuated with — what's her name?
STANLEY (DEXTER). Susan. *(SUSAN reacts, surprised. The others watch her. She will seem uncomfortable.)* I've just met her recently, but I feel like I've known her a long, long time.
DEXTER. Have you asked her for a date?
STANLEY (DEXTER). Not yet. I'm too shy.
DEXTER. Why don't I ask her for you? Susan, would you like to go out with my little friend, Stanley?
SUSAN. Daddy ... *(Beat.)* ... Daddy doesn't allow me to date dummies.

(The others laugh, clap and ad-lib lines like "Good answer, Susan.")

DEXTER. I'm sorry, Stanley. It seems the young lady doesn't return your infatuation.

LUCINDA. I'll go out with you, Stanley. I not only date dummies, I usually marry them!

(Everyone laughs.)

STANLEY (DEXTER). What are you doing Saturday night, sweetie?

DEXTER. Wait a minute! Not so fast! Before I let you go out with Ms. Tate, I need to know something about her. Ms. Tate, tell us about yourself.

(He crosses to the SL end of the sofa and sits with STANLEY on his lap as LUCINDA rises and crosses to DEXTER's spot CS. Everyone applauds DEXTER as they switch places.)

LUCINDA. You want to know about me? Sure, I'll tell you. Lucinda Tate's the name. My life is an open book. It's titled: "In the Garden of Love, I Keep Picking the Stinkweeds." I've had every kind of spouse: the louse, the grouse, the souse and the mouse. The louse was my first husband, Irving. We had the ideal marriage — for about ten minutes. I should have realized something was wrong when he and my maid of honor both disappeared from the reception for over an hour, but I was young and naive. It was two years before I came to realize that Irving was chasing anything in a skirt ... and I had a closet full of slacks. I showed Irving the door; my mistake was letting husband number two, George, come through it — George, the grouse. He groused about everything — my cleaning, my washing, my ironing, my cooking ... my cooking ... my cooking.... Hey, I never claimed to be Betty Crocker. Heck, I can't even keep up with Mrs. Paul. Eventually, I gave George some coupons for fast food restaurants and sent him on his way. That brings us to husband number three, Benny the souse. Benny had a drinking problem. I don't joke about Benny because that kind of problem is no laughing matter. I just mention him to keep the record straight. I'm happy to say he later got help and is doing well. My fourth and latest husband Willard was a mouse. As in

YOU COULD DIE LAUGHING! 59

timid? How timid was he, you ask ....
  ALL EXCEPT JOEY. *(In unison.)* How timid was he?
  LUCINDA. Thank you. Willard was so shy he blushed at the sight of a plucked chicken ... so shy that at parties he'd stand very still in a corner and hope people would mistake him for a statue ... so shy that he kept his socks on when he trimmed his toenails. As you can tell, I'm an out-there kind'a gal, so Willard and I were not what you'd call compatible. I was fire, he was ice, and whenever I got near him, he started to puddle. When he eventually asked me for a divorce, I had to agree it was a good idea. Actually, he didn't "ask" me, he left me a note in my shoe. We untied the knot and went our separate ways. So, Stanley, if you still want a date, look me up when we get back to the states. I'm in the yellow pages under "Desperate."
  CORA. Hey, wait a minute! Lucinda's not the only chicken running free in the pen! I ain't married, and never have been. I want a turn to make my pitch! *(LUCINDA sweeps her arm meaning "be my guest", then returns to her seat as CORA rises and crosses to CS. Everyone applauds LUCINDA as they swap. When she's in place, CORA says:)* Hi, neighbors! It's good ta see ya!
  ALL. *(In unison.)* Hi, Cora!
  CORA. Nothin' warms my heart more than a friendly greetin' ... 'cept Uncle Buford's jalapeno chili grande! *(She touches her chest and mimes burping.)* I don't generally go fer fancy foreign foods, but Buford's chili really turns up my thermostat. So, Stanley, if'n yore looking fer a hot date, let me gulp down some 'a that volcano juice and I'll be ready. Ya know, if'n we hit it off, I'll take ya home to the Ozarks ta meet some 'a my kinfolk. I got some pretty in'erestin' relations. Fer instance, my cousin Lester — Lester's got six toes on each foot. When we wuz kids, he always won when we played kick the can. His twin brother Luther used ta tease Lester 'bout havin' twelve toes in all, but one day while Luther wuz huntin' rabbits, his rifle went off and shot off two 'a his own toes, so then the twins had the rite number between 'em. It jes goes ta show how nicely life balances thangs out sometimes, don't it? I got a bunch 'a other kinfolk you can meet: Cousin Jewel, the alligator woman — she's got real dry skin,

but it got her inta show business, travelin' with a carnival; Aunt Brodie who's a conjure woman — she can boil down a mess 'a wil'fliers and moss and stuff that'll melt a wart right off ya; Uncle P. U. an' his pet skunks …. oh, there's lots more of 'em. You jess say the word, Stanley, an' we'll git ta know each other real well! Yore turn, Antonio.

(CORA returns to her seat as the others applaud.)

ANTONIO. You can skip me — I already told you about my night in a Georgia jail.
JOEY. I decline to perform as well. I never present my material around other comedians —— I have no desire to have my best jokes pop up in someone else's act.
ZOWIE. *(Rising; angry.)* Hey! Are you calling us thieves!?!
JOEY. If the shoe fits ….
ZOWIE. Let's see how well my shoe fits against your backside!
ANTONIO. *(Rising.)* Calm down, Zowie. We've all known for years that Joey thinks he's superior to the rest of us. Ignore him.
ZOWIE. I might as well — the way his audience always did.

(JOEY gives her an angry glare. ZOWIE and ANTONIO sit.)

ANTONIO. Sammy and Paulette, show us what you got.
SAMMY. If you insist. *(Rising.)* Stand up, Paulette.
PAULETTE. *(Rising.)* Are we going somewhere?
SAMMY. *(Taking her hand and leading her to CS.)* Just right down here. We're going to do a routine.
PAULETTE. I forgot to bring my baton.
SAMMY. Not that kind of routine, Paulette — a comedy routine. Tell everyone how we met.
PAULETTE. We met on a blind date. It was love at first sight.
SAMMY. That sounded rather strange, but it was love at first sight for me, too.
PAULETTE. I was talking about you. It took me a few more

glances till I felt it. *(Beat.)* Twelve.

SAMMY. Twelve glances? You remember that?

PAULETTE. Well, sure. A woman always remembers when she falls in love.

SAMMY. What made you fall? My handsome face? Manly physique? Wit? Intelligence? Charm?

PAULETTE. Keep going.

SAMMY. *(Thinking.)* Uh ... uh ....

PAULETTE. It was your smile. You've always had the nicest smile.

SAMMY. Thank you, dear. You've always given me a lot to smile about. You know, we have an anniversary coming up soon. What would you like me to get you?

PAULETTE. A henway.

SAMMY. What's a henway?

PAULETTE. About five pounds. *(Beat.)* That was a little joke.

SAMMY. Yes, dear, and an old one, too. Putting all joking aside ....

PAULETTE. *(Cutting in.)* Oh, we can't do that, Sammy — we wouldn't have an act.

SAMMY. You're right, of course. Anyway, our anniversary's coming up. What gift would you like me to get you?

PAULETTE. A box of candy.

SAMMY. Think bigger than that.

PAULETTE. A big box of candy.

SAMMY. No, Paulette, you're still thinking too small; think ... HUGE!

PAULETTE. A HUGE box of candy!

SAMMY. What I meant is, name something that costs a lot of money. A new car! A fur coat! Diamonds! A trip!

PAULETTE. A trip! I want a trip!

SAMMY. It's yours, dearest. Where would you like to go?

PAULETTE. To Hershey, Pennsylvania; I've heard the candy factory there gives away free samples.

SAMMY. Whatever makes you happy, Paulette.

PAULETTE. That's you, Sammy. You make me happy.

(PAULETTE and SAMMY give each other a sweet little kiss. The others, except JOEY, applaud.)

SAMMY. Colleen.

(SAMMY leads PAULETTE to the window seat where they sit as COLLEEN rises and crosses to CS.)

COLLEEN. Isn't it nice to see a couple who are still in love after having been married for so many years? It makes me feel all choked up.
CORKY. Hey, Colleen, are you sure that's not your cooking?

(The others, except JOEY, laugh.)

COLLEEN. No, smarty. I'm a very good cook. I did have my own show, you know.
CORKY. I know, but .... *(Beat.)* I just remembered ... a long time ago I read something in *Variety* .... Oh, yeah, the article said when you gave your studio audience samples of the lasagna you'd made on the air that day, they ended up in the hospital with stomach cramps.
ZOWIE. Hey, I saw that, too. I had forgot about it.
COLLEEN. I hoped that by now, everyone would have forgot it. Look, it was an accident, okay? I thought I was spraying the baking dish with Pam, but I grabbed another can by mistake.
ANTONIO. What was in the can?
COLLEEN. Insect spray.
SUSAN. You mean you poisoned...!?!

(SUSAN stops when ALLEN puts his hand on her arm. They exchange a look.)

COLLEEN. Well, sort of, but nobody died.

YOU COULD DIE LAUGHING! 63

HELENA. I guess that makes it one of your more successful dishes.

(The others laugh nervously.)

LUCINDA. *(Softly, to CORA.)* You notice she didn't mention that little boo-boo when we were talking about grabbing the wrong cans yesterday?

CORA. Uh-huh.

COLLEEN. Well, anyway, I don't want to talk about lasagna, I want to talk about turkeys.

CORKY. Hey, Antonio, Colleen's gonna talk about you.

COLLEEN. Shut up, Corky. Pretend I'm taping my cooking show. The subject for today is "Take Your Turkey and Stuff It." Many families have a turkey for dinner only once a year at Thanksgiving ....

ANTONIO. *(Cutting in.)* Every meal at my house was a turkey; Mama is a lousy cook.

COLLEEN. Thank you for sharing that with us, Antonio. I'm sure if your mother had watched my show, that would not have been the case. Now, as I was saying, turkey and dressing is an entree that can be enjoyed throughout the year, not just on special occasions, because it doesn't have to be difficult to prepare. The first thing you do is buy a nice, plumb turkey.

CORA. If'n we wuz lucky enough to have turkey when I wuz a kid, the first thing we had to do wuz shoot it.

COLLEEN. *(Growing exasperated.)* Well, however you obtain it, let's jump ahead to where you're ready to cook the little sucker, okay!?! *(ANTONIO and CORA murmur "okay.")* Fine. Before you do anything else, pre-heat the oven to 325 degrees ... or in Cora's case, put two sticks of kindling into the stove and light them. Next, put your hand inside the turkey and pull out the giblets.

HELENA. You stick your hand inside a turkey's rump and pull out its innerds? Oh, gross!

COLLEEN. Relax, Helena — they seal the giblets in a bag at the packing plant.

HELENA. Oh. That's not so bad, then.

COLLEEN. You can tell who knows their way around the kitchen in this crowd. As I said, take out the bag of giblets. If you don't, you'll be sorry. I forgot to take the bag out one time, and it caught fire. I had the only turkey on the block that was burned on the inside and raw on the outside. Usually, it's the other way around ... if your oven's too hot, that it. While we're on the subject, you'll want to bake your bird for thirty minutes per pound. If you don't know how much the turkey weighs, it's easy to find out. Strip naked and step on your scales, holding your turkey. Then set it down. The difference between the two readings is how much your turkey weighs.

CORKY. *(To ANTONIO.)* I hope she doesn't try that method in the supermarket.

COLLEEN. Now, back to your stuffing. Make a pan of cornbread the day before and don't touch it for twenty-four hours.

ANTONIO. That would'a worked at my house. Mama tried making cornbread once and nobody touched it for a month. She finally threw it out to the birds; they threw it back at her.

COLLEEN. Who's routine is this anyway!?!

ANTONIO. Sorry.

COLLEEN. Crumble the cornbread into a bowl. Next add chopped celery, onion, spices, a can of condensed chicken broth, and mix it all up together with your hands.

HELENA. Yuck!

COLLEEN. I agree with the great cook Julia Child; she said the best cooking utensils in your kitchen are your hands.

ZOWIE. I'd like to see her flip pancakes with them. *(COLLEEN shoots her a look.)* Just an observation ....

COLLEEN. Once your stuffing is mixed well, scoop it up by the handsful and stick it into the turkey. Take your bird by its legs and shake it to settle the stuffing — do not pack it in. After you've done that, take a needle and a length of cord and sew up the opening.

CORKY. You're kidding, right?

COLLEEN. I certainly am not. That's the proper method to seal in the flavor.

CORKY. So where did you learn to cook? At Johns Hopkins University's Medical School? *(Pretending to be a doctor:)* "Scalpel! Clamps! Cornbread stuffing! Quickly, nurse! The fate of this turkey is in your hands!" *(With a nurse voice:)* "Yes, doctor, but I think we're wasting our time. In case you haven't noticed, the patient's head has been chopped off!"

COLLEEN. That's it, Corky! You're going to need a doctor if you don't stop interrupting!

CORKY. *(Making a palms-out "sorry" gesture.)* Carry on.

COLLEEN. There's not much left. Place the turkey into your oven — in a pan, of course — and bake it, basting the bird occasionally with a turkey baster.

ZOWIE. *(A whisper to HELENA.)* Or — if you're Julia Child — with your hand.

COLLEEN. Stir up some giblet gravy, serve, and enjoy. Thank you. *(All except JOEY applaud.)* Since you're so eager to perform, Corky, be my guest.

(COLLEEN returns to her seat and CORKY rises and crosses to CS as some of the others ad-lib "Go, Corky", "All right!", etc.)

CORKY. Not Corky. You're looking at Rick Danger, private investigator. *(He assumes the demeanor of hard-boiled detective in the manner of Humphrey Bogart in the movie "The Maltese Falcon".)* Let me tell you about my latest case. I call it "The Latest Case." It was midnight. A Thursday. I was working late, the only one left in my office building. I was startled by a noise in the hallway — footsteps — click, click, click. Obviously a woman in high heels. I knew it wasn't my secretary, Daisy, 'cause she always wears sandals. When she walks, they go flop-flop-flop. There was a knock at my door. Rap-rap-rap. I said, "Come in" and she did — all of her. Lana Luscious was a knockout — six feet tall with long blonde hair, big blue eyes, full red lips ... the ears and nose weren't bad either — and that's just her head. She had a body that would stick out in any crowd, if you know what I mean. I stood up. "Can I help you?" I asked. "I hope so, Mr. Danger," she replied. "I'm Lana Luscious. Someone is trying to kill me." "How can you be sure?" I asked. "Because he's coming down the hall with a gun," she answered. Sure enough, at that moment this big goon appeared right behind her. "Hit the floor!" I yelled as I pulled my .38 from my shoulder holster. She did. Splat. Goonface was holding a .45, pointed straight at me. He fired. I fired. He missed. I didn't. He dropped to the floor right beside Lana Luscious. Really big splat. I came around the desk and helped Lana up. "You're safe now," I said. "The guy's dead." "Thanks, pal," she said. "I owe you one — and I always pay my debts." Then she planted a kiss on me that would melt a fireman's rubber boot. When I could catch my breath, I asked, "Did you know the dead guy?" "I've seen him around," she answered. "He's my husband." "Why did he want to kill you?" I asked. "He was insanely jealous," Lana said, "always accusing me of seeing other men. I told him he was imagining it, but he didn't believe me. Well, gotta go, Rick — I'm late for a date." I asked, "Who with?" "The Miami Dolphins," she answered, and wiggled out the door. As it turned out, the late Mr. Luscious had a pretty shady past, so the cops didn't give me too hard a time for plugging him. I never saw Lana Luscious again, but you'll find me in my office most midnights, just in case.... *(He nods and says:)* Helena.

(The others, except JOEY, applaud as he returns to his seat and HELENA rises and crosses to CS.)

HELENA. Nice characterization, Corky. Me, I don't do characters. I just talk ... about my views, my experiences, my life in general. Hey — let's be specific — I usually talk about what it's like to be a single woman in a couple-driven society. Actually, I don't mind being single all that much — it's my mother who takes another step closer to Looneyville each time I pass another birthday unmarried. In my early twenties, she introduced me to handsome, smart young men with bright futures. Now she encourages me to walk down any dark alley I come across in hopes I'll meet a street person who's not too picky.

For a while she called a different pizza place every night and had them deliver a pizza to my house. She said if one of the delivery men and I hit it off, at least I would marry a man who made sure I never go hungry. She finally quit after I told her I had gained fifteen pounds, and the only unattached delivery people I had met were a sixteen-year-old boy named Ralph and a woman named Brenda. I'm still trying to work off those pepperonis which went right to my thighs. Mom still hasn't given up, though. Every night she calls and asks me the same question: "Darling, did you meet Mr. Wonderful today?" "No, Mom, I met Mr. Super-ego, Mr. Mama's Boy and a couple of Mr. Potato Heads." She says that where men are concerned, my standards are too high. Well, I'm sorry, but I insist that any potential husband of mine must be able to read words with more than five letters, eat soup without dribbling on himself and be able to breathe without the help of a respirator. If those standards are too high, then Mom will just have to deal with it. I'm happy to say that last week I met a single guy who met two out of the three criteria. Who knows? -- if my luck continues to improve, I just might meet the man for me any day now. *(She nods.)* Zowie, it's all yours.

(The others except JOEY applaud as she returns to her seat and ZOWIE rises and crosses to CS.)

ZOWIE. You might recall that a few years ago, I starred as Sister Fabiola in my own TV series, "Simply Divine." After two seasons, when our ratings went from lukewarm straight to hell, if you'll pardon the expression, it was obvious we were going to be cancelled. I hoped for divine intervention, but a miracle didn't happen. Sister Fab got the ax. Since then, I've had quite a bit of time on my hands, and I found myself watching a lot of television. The individual shows weren't that hot, but I discovered that TV can be a hoot if you become a channel surfer. Imagine flipping between old movie stations, commercials and a soap and you get something like this:

*** ZOWIE'S ROUTINE ***

(During her monologue, ZOWIE will play several characters, changing her voice for each. She will stand in one spot, but will help delineate between the movies, commercials and soap by angling her body slightly left for the movie characters, face front for the commercial actors, and angle slightly right for the soap characters.)

MOVIES/COMMERCIALS/SOAP

GANGSTER. *(Angry.)* Okay, Eddie, ya dirty rat! Ya squealed on me! Ya know what I'm gonna do about that!?! I'm gonna ...

FIRST PITCH WOMAN. *(Soothing voice.)* ... guarantee you'll never be troubled with constipation again.

GANGSTER. *(Mimes shooting Tommy gun.)* Ak! Ak! Ak! Ak! Ak!...

FIRST SOAP ACTRESS. Was that the doorbell? *(Mimes opening door.)* Yes? Oh, Evelyn.... What's the matter? You look like...

MALE CHARACTER IN MONSTER MOVIE. ...Godzilla! It's going to destroy Tokyo if you don't ...

FIRST SOAP ACTRESS. ...come in and have a cup of ...

FIRST PITCH MAN. ... Drano! It's guaranteed to clean your pipes!

SECOND SOAP ACTRESS. Thank you, Marsha, but I need something stronger. Do you have any ...

SECOND PITCH WOMAN. Kool-Aid! It's not just for kids, it's for ...

FEMALE CHARACTER IN SCI-FI MOVIE. ... giant grasshoppers! Can we stop them!?!

MALE CHARACTER. I don't know, Shirley! It depends ....

THIRD PITCH WOMAN. *(Mimes holding up box.)* Depends!

FIRST SOAP ACTRESS. ...depends on what you mean by missing, Evelyn. How long has Jason been gone?

SECOND SOAP ACTRESS. Three days! Oh, Marsha, I suspect he ran off with ...

SPORTS ANNOUNCER. ... the winners of the Women's Vol-

YOU COULD DIE LAUGHING! 69

leyball Competition! Sunday! At 8:00 P. M.!

FEMALE CHARACTER IN DRAMA. Look! There on the beach! It's his body! *(She screams.)*

SECOND SOAP ACTRESS.) *(Turns scream into sobs.)* What am I going to do, Marsha? I'm about to lose my ...

FOURTH PITCH WOMAN. Cheerios!

FIRST SOAP ACTRESS. You're jumping to conclusions, Evelyn. Jason might have been in an accident -- hit by a car. He could be lying in a hospital bed with ...

SECOND PITCH MAN. ... bad breath....

FEMALE CHARACTER IN LOVE STORY. Kiss me! Kiss me! I love you, Reginald, and I'll always be your ...

FIFTH PITCH WOMAN. Pop tart!

FIRST SOAP ACTRESS. You don't mean that, Evelyn. You'd forgive Jason, no matter what he's done, because down deep in your heart you know ...

THIRD PITCH MAN. You're in good hands with All State.

SECOND SOAP ACTRESS. Thank you for your wonderful advice, Marsha. I don't know what I'd do without you. You're a ...

SIXTH PITCH WOMAN. Lifesaver!

SECOND SOAP ACTRESS. I'll leave now....

ACTRESS WITH A SOUTHERN ACCENT. Yes, go! Go before the Yankees come to burn down the plantation!

FOURTH PITCH MAN. Do you have adequate fire insurance?

FIRST SOAP ACTRESS. Goodbye, Evelyn. Wait patiently. I'm sure Jason will return.

SECOND SOAP ACTRESS. Yes ... yes, I will. Goodbye, Marsha.

FIRST SOAP ACTRESS. *(Beat.)* You can come out now, Jason. She's gone.

*** END OF ROUTINE ***

(ZOWIE bows and returns to her seat as everyone, except JOEY, applauds.)

JOEY. Is that it? Everyone's best shot?

ZOWIE. Yeah, and we'd better not hear any of our material in your act!

JOEY. I can assure you I wouldn't take any of those jokes if you gave them to me.

HELENA. So — what do we do now?

LUCINDA. *(Rising.)* I don't know about the rest of you, but I'm ready to take my cocoa to my room and try to get some sleep.

CORA. Are you hopin' yore dream lover will show up again?

LUCINDA. You never know. What time is it? *(She looks at the clock.)* Twelve-forty? *(She says the actual time on the clock.)* It's way past my bedtime.

ALLEN. *(Looking at his watch and frowning.)* It's later than that — it's one a.m.

ZOWIE. The clock must be losing time. I'll set it.

SUSAN. I got it.

(SUSAN rises, turns to face the clock, opens its door, moves the hands to 1:00, then closes it.)

ALLEN. *(Frowning.)* It's strange that the clock.... Never mind. Maybe the gears need oiling. I'll check it in the morning.

SAMMY. *(Rising.)* I think Lucinda's got the right idea. Come on, Paulette, let's get some shut-eye.

PAULETTE. All right, dear.

(PAULETTE rises, then shuts her eyes and starts to feel her way UL.)

SAMMY. I meant AFTER we go to bed.

PAULETTE. Whatever you say.

(SAMMY takes her hand. They start UL.)

ANTONIO. *(Rising.)* I know this goes without saying, but I'll say it anyway: everybody lock your doors.

YOU COULD DIE LAUGHING! 71

(SAMMY and PAULETTE turn back to listen.)

CORKY. *(Rising.)* Lock 'em? I'm thinking about going to the shed, finding a hammer and some nails and nailing mine shut!
HELENA. *(Rising.)* I don't think you have to go that far, Corky. All our bedrooms are close together. If anyone needs help, just yell out and the rest of us will come running.

(Anyone else still seated rises.)

STANLEY (DEXTER). I might have a problem with that — yelling or running.
SUSAN. I guess we all should try to get some sleep. Maybe tomorrow we can find a way to get off this island — or, at least, summon help.

(The others ad-lib agreement and start UL, carrying their mugs.)

COLLEEN. Wait, everyone! This is important! *(All turn to look at her.)* If you're taking your cocoa to your rooms, be sure to find something to use as coasters for your mugs. We don't want to make rings on any of M. St. Yves' lovely furniture, do we?
HELENA. *(Sarcastic.)* Heavens, no, Colleen! I'd rather die first! *(The others react and HELENA realizes what she said. With a weak smile and an apologetic gesture.)* Just kidding ....

(All continue to exit except ALLEN who has lagged behind. Once he's alone, he crosses to the clock, opens the door, takes hold of the pendulum, stopping it. His fingers touch the backside of the pendulum. He holds a beat, smiles to himself. He takes a ring of keys from his pocket and begins to search through them. The lights fade to Blackout.
In the darkness, ALLEN puts the keys back into his pocket, starts the pendulum swinging, closes the clock door, crosses to the window seat, takes the flashlight SAMMY left there and climbs into the window seat. A STAGEHAND sets the clock to 2:50.)

Scene 2

(Two hours later, about 3:00 a.m.)

Pale moonlight fades up outside the window. After a beat, a FIGURE enters off UL, crosses behind the window, and enters UC. It wears a rain slicker like the men wore in the previous scene, black pants, gloves and a black knit ski mask under the slicker's hood. It carries a lighted flashlight and a gasoline can. We can't tell if it's a man or a woman. It circles the room, pouring gasoline [water] from the can onto the floor, ending at the mantle. It sets down the can. ALLEN raises the lid of the window seat stealthily and watches. The FIGURE opens the clock door and stops the pendulum. It removes something from behind the pendulum, closes the door and puts the object into its pocket. It picks up the can, crosses DL and exits. ALLEN climbs from the window seat, switches on the flashlight, and hurries silently to the door DL. Just before he reaches it, there are two screams from the kitchen which makes him freeze a beat before he starts to lunge toward the door again. As he reaches it, LUCINDA and CORA charge out the door DL and collide with ALLEN, causing all three to cry out. The women wear nightclothes, robes and house slippers.)

ALLEN. *(Shining his light on their faces.)* Cora! Lucinda!

LUCINDA. *(Clinging to him, frightened out of her wits.)* Who's Lucinda!?! Oh, I'm Lucinda! He!... She!... It's in there!

CORA. *(Equally scared; also clinging to him.)* It's a ghost! I know a haint when I see one! It's Mr. Thorn's ghost come back to haunt us!

ALLEN. Nonsense! It's the killer! *(LUCINDA and CORA let out loud screams, terrified, and cling to ALLEN even tighter.)* Let me see who ....

LUCINDA. Don't leave me! Don't leave me! Oh my gosh, I feel like I'm pleading with my third husband! Talk about *déjà vu* ...

(COLLEEN runs in UL, holding a box of tissues over her head like a

YOU COULD DIE LAUGHING! 73

club in one hand, a candle in the other. She wears a nightgown and house slippers. She flips on the light switch by the UL door. The lights come up.)

COLLEEN. Who screamed!?! What's going on!?!
ALLEN. Put out the candle! There's gas on the floor! Stay here!

(ALLEN breaks free and runs out DL. COLLEEN blows out the candle, then crosses to LUCINDA and CORA who now cling to each other.)

COLLEEN. What on earth happened?
ZOWIE. We saw Mr. Thorn's ghost!
LUCINDA. Or the killer! Take your pick!
COLLEEN. Those are my choices? I don't want to meet up with either one!

(ANTONIO and CORKY run in. ANTONIO wears very loud boxer shorts, a t-shirt and white socks. CORKY wears pajamas.)

ANTONIO & CORKY. Who screamed!?!
LUCINDA & CORA. I did.
COLLEEN. They did. I grabbed the first thing I could get my hands on and rushed downstairs when I heard them. I was going to try to protect them.
ANTONIO. With a box of Kleenex? What were you going to do if you came face to face with the killer? Fluff him to death?
CORA. She couldn't come face ta face with him 'cause it didn't have a face! There wuz a black hole where its head should'a been! It wuz a ghost!

(ALLEN enters DL holding the rain coat and a black ski mask, his flashlight and the gas can.)

ALLEN. No, it was the killer — wearing a ski mask and Mr. Thorn's raincoat. This stuff was on the kitchen floor. *(He crosses to the table DR and lays the coat and mask there, along with his flashlight. He sets the gas can on the floor.)* I looked into the Thorns' room to see if the intruder had ducked in there. No luck — he got away. But I noticed this rain coat was missing from the floor where we laid it when we took it off Mr. Thorn before we put him on the bed.

    ANTONIO. *(As he and CORKY cross to ALLEN DR.)* That's right, we did.

    CORKY. Apparently, the bad guy took it to use as a disguise.

    ALLEN. So it seems.

(COLLEEN leads CORA and LUCINDA to the sofa and seats them. She sits on the chair DL of it.)

    CORA. Then I guess it wasn't a ghost after all.

    ANTONIO. I can think of something worse than Mr. Thorn's ghost roaming around the house, though.

    COLLEEN. What's that?

    ANTONIO. Mrs. Thorn's ghost.

    CORKY. No argument. *(Sniffing.)* Allen, did you spill gas from that can?

    ALLEN. No, the killer doused the floor with it.

    CORKY. Why? You think he was planning to turn us into toast?

    ALLEN. That would be my guess.

    ANTONIO. Heavy!

(ZOWIE and HELENA enter UL. They wear nightclothes. HELENA has green goop on her face — a beauty mask — and curlers under a hairnet on her head.)

    ZOWIE. What's happening!?!

(CORKY turns to them, sees HELENA and yelps.)

    CORKY. It's the Creature from the Black Lagoon!

    HELENA. I'll get you for that, Corky!

YOU COULD DIE LAUGHING! 75

CORKY. Helena?

HELENA. Of course. This is a beauty mask. I want to look my best if we live through this and I get to meet M. St. Yves.

CORKY. You just better hope he never sees you like that or he'll hire you to host a Monster Madness show.

ANTONIO. You should have known it wasn't the Creature from the Black Lagoon, Corky. Helena's wearing curlers and the Creature didn't have any hair.

ZOWIE. *(Crossing to UC.)* Would somebody please tell us what the yelling was about before I start doing some of my own!?!

HELENA. *(Crossing to ZOWIE.)* And it had better be good!

(SAMMY and PAULETTE enter UL in nightclothes.)

COLLEEN. Allen, Cora and Lucinda saw the killer.

HELENA. That's good enough.

ZOWIE. I'd yell.

SAMMY. The killer? You saw the killer? Who ...?

ALLEN. Couldn't tell. He was wearing this ... *(Picking up the coat)* ... or she.

PAULETTE. I can't imagine why any woman would ever wear a coat like that — the shape and color would make all of us look terribly overweight with a sallow complexion.

ZOWIE. I doubt if murderesses care about displaying good fashion sense, Paulette.

HELENA. What's that smell?

LUCINDA. Gas.

PAULETTE. Beg pardon.

JOEY. *(Entering UL. He wears expensive pajamas and a silk robe.)* What's happened now? Has yet another body shown up?

ZOWIE. No, and don't look so hopeful, Joey — none of your competition has been bumped off yet.

JOEY. Competition? What competition? I assume there's a reason for all the commotion?

ALLEN. Cora and Lucinda got a scare, but they're okay.

LUCINDA. If you count having ten years taken off your life okay.
PAULETTE. I wouldn't mind being ten years younger.
SAMMY. Let's sit down, dear.

(He leads her to the window seat where they sit.)

JOEY. It's just a guess, but did the ladies' scare have anything to do with Helena's appearance?
HELENA. Watch it, Joey! At least MY beauty routine doesn't include a plastic surgeon.

(JOEY shoots her a look.)

SAMMY. What did frighten Cora and Lucinda?
ANTONIO. The killer was just prowling around the lodge. They saw him ... or her. The person was wearing that stuff.

(ANTONIO points to DR table.)

SAMMY. Is everyone all right?
CORA. I s'pose so. Who's not here?
ALLEN. *(Realizing.)* Susan! Where's Susan!?!

(ALLEN takes a step toward UL but stops as SUSAN enters there, limping slightly. She is wearing nightclothes and a robe.)

SUSAN. I'm here. I jumped out of bed when I heard screams and banged my knee on the bedpost. My knee hurts like crazy. Who screamed? What happened?
CORA. I wuz havin' trouble gettin' ta sleep, so I knocked on Lucinda's door an' asked her ta come down to the kitchen with me fer a glass 'a warm milk. I didn't want ta come by myself.
LUCINDA. I was happy to accompany Cora, even though when she woke me, I was having a fantastic dream; it involved me, Harrison Ford *(or name any attractive leading man)* and a kiddie pool filled

YOU COULD DIE LAUGHING! 77

with raspberry Jell-O. Anyway, we came down the servants' stairs in the back, and walked into the kitchen ....

CORA. *(Cutting in.)* ... when somebody wearin' that raincoat an' ski mask came in through that there door! Lucinda an' me flew in here like buzzards with their tail feathers on fire!

LUCINDA. And ran right into Allen.

SUSAN. You saw the figure, too, Allen?

ALLEN. Yeah.

SUSAN. What was it doing?

ALLEN. Pouring gasoline on the floor. I assume it intended to incinerate us. I'll keep an eye out down here while the rest of you get dressed. We need to get out of the lodge. It's a bonfire ready to be ignited.

PAULETTE. Does that mean we can't go back to sleep?

HELENA. Sleep? "MacBeth hath murdered sleep."

ANTONIO. Say what?

HELENA. Shakespeare. I took some acting classes when I was younger.

COLLEEN. You never told me that. I'm impressed.

HELENA. I'm glad you are; the teacher wasn't. Once I did Lady MacBeth in a scene study exercise. I figured, "Hey, this woman is so fiery and hot-tempered, maybe the Big Mac had married an Italian gal, so I played her with an accent. When I said, "Out-a, out-a damned-a spot-a!" my teacher, Mr. Kline, nearly croaked.

CORKY. An Italian Lady MacBeth? How were you going to top that, Helena? Play Ophelia as the girlfriend of Hamlet, Prince of Denmark and Newark, New Jersey? There'd be a great chance to use another accent — *(As Ophelia with a Jersey accent:)* "Geeze, Hamlet, youse don't look so good. I heard youse was cholicky; maybe dat's why dey call you 'Duh Cholicky Dane.'"

HELENA. He's called "The Melancholy Dane," nitwit, and I don't need your help to tank my acting career — I managed to do that on my own. From now on, I'm sticking to stand-up comedy where I belong.

ZOWIE. You hang in there, girlfriend!

ALLEN. I believe you were going to get dressed?

CORKY. Oh, yeah.... Hey, wait a minute! We're still missing

somebody! Dexter! Where's Dexter?

(The others ad-lib, realizing CORKY's right. DEXTER, carrying STANLEY, enters from off UR and comes in UC. He wears jeans, a Western shirt, hat and boots, and has a holster with two guns strapped to his waist. STANLEY is dressed in similar attire and has a pair of kid's cap pistols in a holster around his waist.)

DEXTER. I'm here, dear boy.
CORA. Dexter! What were you doing outside — and dressed like an extra out of an old Roy Rogers movie?
DEXTER. Well ... I ....
STANLEY (DEXTER). Tell them, Dexter. It's okay.
DEXTER. Well, a little while ago I was awakened by someone tapping softly on my door.
STANLEY (DEXTER). Dexter's a light sleeper. I sleep like a log.
DEXTER. I turned on the light and saw a piece of paper being slipped under the door. By the time I got to the door and opened it, the hallway was empty.
STANLEY (DEXTER). I didn't see anyone either.
COLLEEN. What did the note say?
DEXTER. It said I should get dressed and go quietly to the plane without telling anyone.
STANLEY (DEXTER). It said to wait there and we'd be taken off the island. We grabbed the first clothes we could find.
DEXTER. Actually, I think it said I would.
STANLEY (DEXTER). Technically, but everyone knows that I go where you go.
ZOWIE. Who signed it?
DEXTER. It just said "a friend."
JOEY. Where's the note?
DEXTER. I don't know. I suppose I left it in our room.
JOEY. Hogwash! My guess is you're the one who poured gasoline on the floor and was going to burn the lodge to the ground with

YOU COULD DIE LAUGHING! 79

the rest of us trapped upstairs! Then you'd be the only comedian left to star in M. St. Yves' TV show! And, frankly, I think it's the only way you'd be chosen!

(The others ad-lib, some dubious, some agreeing reluctantly.)

DEXTER. Gasoline? I knew I smelled something, don't you, Stanley?

STANLEY (DEXTER). Nope — my sinuses are completely blocked up.

ALLEN. *(Crossing to him.)* This isn't the time for jokes, Mr. Porter. We're leaving now. I have the key to the plane.

SAMMY. You do? Where did you find it?

ALLEN. It was taped to the back of the pendulum in the clock. I figured that out earlier tonight. When we got here yesterday, the clock was working perfectly — I compared its time with my watch. Later, when it began to lose minutes, I wondered what would slow it down. That's when it occurred to me that something could be attached to the pendulum — something small, like my missing key.

ZOWIE. That's why you said you'd take a look at the clock tomorrow — I mean, later today. You figured the killer would have to come down after we had all gone to bed to retrieve it.

ALLEN. You got it, Zowie. After the rest of you went up to bed earlier, I swapped the airplane key for the key to my post office mail box, then I hid in the window seat and waited. A few minutes ago, the killer showed up with the gas can. I was going to follow the culprit to his room, discover his identity, then quietly gather the rest of you and fly you off the island, stranding the killer here.

ZOWIE. That is so cool! You're better than that dorky detective in the show I guest starred on!

LUCINDA. Your plan would have worked, too, if Cora and I hadn't spoiled it.

ALLEN. No, Lucinda, it's not your fault. Mr. Porter's attempt to burn down the lodge changed everything.

PAULETTE. I feel like Snow White in the forest.

SAMMY. What do you mean, dear?
PAULETTE. I'm totally lost.
SAMMY. I'll explain it later, Paulette ... if I ever figure it out.
LUCINDA. Wait a minute — how do we know Dexter is really the killer?
ALLEN. Because of these.... *(He grabs the guns from DEXTER's holster.)* I'll take the guns, Mr. Porter.... *(Surprised.)* They're toys!
CORA. What did you expect, Allen?
ALLEN. I kept it quiet, but the killer got his hands on two guns — one from the plane and Mr. Thorn's. I thought ....
SUSAN. *(Pulling a gun from her robe pocket with her right hand.)* I believe this is what you were looking for, Allen. Move away from Daddy.
COLLEEN. Daddy!?!

(All ad-lib, surprised and confused. ALLEN steps back from DEXTER.)

SUSAN. *(Brandishing the gun.)* All of you move where I can see you.

(CORKY, ANTONIO, ALLEN, JOEY and ZOWIE cross to SR. LUCINDA, CORA, HELENA, COLLEEN, SAMMY and PAULETTE cross to SL.)

DEXTER. I don't understand ....
PAULETTE. That's my line. That's always my line.
SUSAN. *(Crossing to DEXTER. They are alone UC.)* I know you don't know me, Daddy, but you will. We're going to catch up on all those years we've been apart.
DEXTER. Susan...? You're my Susan...?
SUSAN. Yes, Daddy.
STANLEY (DEXTER). You're my sister?
SUSAN. *(Furious.)* Never! I was never your sister! You're just a block of wood! I hate you! I've always hated you!
ALLEN. What's this all about, Susan?

SUSAN. *(We begin to realize that she in not quite sane.)* I'm going to make Daddy a big star again! He was a big star when I was a little girl!

(DEXTER's demeanor grows heavy as he begins to feel overwhelmed by the realization of who SUSAN is ... and what she's done.)

DEXTER. Susan ... Susan's mother left me when Susan was five years old ....
SUSAN. And you kept him — Stanley — with you! Why didn't you keep me, too, Daddy?
DEXTER. I couldn't ... my career.... I was always on the road ....
SUSAN. That's not the reason! I know the reason! You loved him best! But you're going to love me best, Daddy, when I make you a star again!
HELENA. You were ... you were going to murder all of us ....
SUSAN. You mean I AM going to murder all of you! I hoped several of you would eat the mints I poisoned — I knew Daddy wouldn't touch them because he's been diabetic since he was a child — but you didn't. Only that old fool, Mr. Thorn, ate them.
ALLEN. Why did you kill Mrs. Thorn?
SUSAN. She saw me with the arsenic. I was carrying the box through the kitchen to the back door to return it to the shed, after I put some on the mints, when she came in from her room. She demanded to know what I was doing with the rat poison. We struggled, and I strangled her with the cord to the mixer.
JOEY. And put the body into the window seat ....
SUSAN. It seemed like the perfect place.
DEXTER. How did you find me after all these years?
SUSAN. I've followed your career all my life, even if Mother wouldn't let me contact you. I knew you live in New York, so I trained to become an airline hostess and was able to get based there. It was the perfect job — I flew a few days a week, even fewer after M. St. Yves hired me. On my days off I would sit in the cafe across the

street from your brownstone. I followed you when you came out for trips to the market or a walk in Central Park ... where ever you went.

DEXTER. When I sensed I was being looked at, I thought it was fans ....

SUSAN. It was! It was me! Your biggest fan!

DEXTER. Why didn't you come to me? Tell me who you are?

SUSAN. Because I didn't have anything to offer you, Daddy! Not till now!

DEXTER. You had yourself.

SUSAN. *(Angry.)* That's not enough! It wasn't enough before!

DEXTER. Oh, Susan ....

SUSAN. *(Excited again.)* But now I can give you your career back! That's something Stanley couldn't do! On one flight, M. St. Yves was working on a list of comics he wanted to audition for a TV show. I told him about you — without letting him know you're my father, of course — and persuaded him to add you to it. I was so happy, Daddy! I knew you'd be proud of me! Then I realized if I made sure you got the series, you'd love me — you'd love me more than you ever loved Stanley!

JOEY. And that's when you decided to knock us off — get rid of the competition?

SUSAN. Yes. I hadn't intended to kill you, too, Allen. I like you — I really do. After I sent Daddy to the plane, I planned to retrieve the key and give it to you — tell you I had found it. Then I was going to find an excuse to get you out of the lodge before I set fire to it. You could have flown Daddy and me back to the mainland. The police would never know who the killer was, even if they suspected Daddy or me. As it is, you'll have to die with the others. After the lodge has burned to the ground, I'll dig up the cell phone batteries where I buried them and call M. St. Yves. He'll send someone to us.

JOEY. *(Putting his hands into his robe pockets.)* You're completely mad!

SUSAN. *(Pointing the gun at him.)* Careful! Keep your hands where I can see them — all of you! *(JOEY takes his hands out of his pockets.)* I got this gun from the plane, Allen, but I don't know who

has the one that was taken from Mr. Thorn's room. If any of you has it on you, I'll shoot you dead before you could pull it out!
    DEXTER. *(Crosses down to behind the sofa; sadly.)* Oh, Susan.... My little girl ....
    SUSAN. *(Crossing to RC, opposite him.)* Don't be sad, Daddy. Everything will be all right ... now .....
    DEXTER. Put the gun down, Susan.
    SUSAN. *(Angry.)* I can't do that! I have to finish what I started! *(Turning to ANTONIO and CORKY, SR.)* Antonio! Corky! Take the mints out of the plastic bags! *(They hesitate.)* Now!

(Each takes a bowl from the mantle and removes it from its plastic bag.)

    COLLEEN. You're not going to ....
    SUSAN. It's the best way! I'm sure you'd all rather die quickly, like Mr. Thorn. Then the fire will destroy all the evidence. That way, we'll tell the police that Daddy and I were the only ones to escape when a fire broke out. When the other gas cans for the generator explode, there won't be anything left for them to examine but ashes. Antonio, take your mints over there.

(SUSAN indicates SL. ANTONIO crosses to the group SL.)

    DEXTER. *(Pleading.)* Susan, don't ....
    SUSAN. Shut up, Daddy! I'm doing this for you! *(To the others.)* Take some mints!

(With trepidation, all but SUSAN and DEXTER take mints from the bowls.)

    DEXTER. You don't know what you're doing ....
    SUSAN. Yes, I do! I know exactly what I'm doing! Eat the mints!

(The others slowly raise their hands with the mints to their faces, terrified.)

DEXTER. *(In total anguish.)* I can't let you do this!

SUSAN. You can't stop me, Daddy!

DEXTER. I'm sorry, Susan .... *(There is a gunshot from inside STANLEY. SUSAN looks startled, turns to DEXTER. He puts STANLEY on the SR end of the sofa, if possible with STANLEY's right arm on the sofa arm, outstretched. DEXTER brings up the hand that was inside STANLEY; a gun is in it. He steps SR to between SUSAN and STANLEY. The others take a step or two toward SUSAN and DEXTER.)* I had to do it.... *(CORA steps down to behind the SR end of the sofa, gripping its back, her hands behind STANLEY.)* I took the gun from the Thorns' room.

SUSAN. *(As if unable to comprehend it; extends her left hand toward DEXTER.)* You shot me ....

(SUSAN slumps to the floor, dead.)

STANLEY (DEXTER). You shot me, too....

(CORA gasps and steps back a step. When she moves, she jars STANLEY so that he slumps against the sofa arm; it looks as if he's extending his arm to DEXTER the same way SUSAN did.)

DEXTER. My children ... I've killed both my children ....

(DEXTER drops the gun, brings his hands to his face, and begins to cry quietly. CORA crosses to him and gathers him into her arms. He sobs against her shoulder.)

HELENA. *(Quietly, to ZOWIE.)* I told you ventriloquists were weird.

(The lights fade to blackout.)

CURTAIN

YOU COULD DIE LAUGHING!

PROPERTY LIST

PRE-SET:

A stagehand presets the clock hands before various scenes
Between Act I, Scenes 2 & 3: Dress material in window seat
Between Acts: Bag one mint dish

PERSONAL:

Firewood - Mr. Thorn
2 candy dishes/mints - Mrs. Thorn
Duffel bags, purses, vanity kits - Cast except the Thorns
Watch - Allen
Luggage - Mr. Thorn
Apron, ladle - Colleen
Knife - Mrs. Thorn
Cup/coffee - Colleen
Cell phones - Susan, Paulette, Zowie
Ziplock bag - Zowie
Rubber gloves - Helena
Tray/pot of cocoa/mugs - Susan
Flashlights - Men except Mr. Thorn
Ring of keys - Allen
Ski mask - Killer
Gas can/water - Killer
Flashlight - Killer
Flashlight (left on window seat) - Allen
Box/tissues - Colleen
Rain coat, ski mask, flashlight, gas can - Allen
Beauty mask, hairnet, curlers - Helena
Holster, cap pistols - Dexter
Gun/blanks - Dexter
Gun - Susan

COSTUME PLOT

Yellow rain coats with hoods in closet for men (except Mr. Thorn)

Act I, Scene 1:

Mr. Thorn - dirty work clothes
Mrs. Thorn - black dress
Allen - pilot's uniform
Susan - flight attendant's uniform
Cora - old-fashioned looking dress, calico or gingham
Helena - chic pants suit
Joey - slacks, open neck shirt, sports coat
Dexter - conservative suit
Stanley - kid's outfit
Antonio - modern, funky clothes
Corky - loud clothes, maybe plaid pants and print shirt
Zowie - casual clothes, maybe baggy pants and t-shirt
Lucinda - wild, bright clothes
Sammy - slacks, turtleneck shirt, sports coat
Paulette - dress
Colleen - summer dress, full skirt, maybe floral
Cast (except Thorns) - lightweight coats, jackets

Between Act I, Scenes 1 & 2:

Cast removes outerwear

Act I, Scene 3:

Mr. Thorn - yellow rain coat with hood

Act II, Scene 2:

Cora - nightclothes, robe, house shoes

SET DRAWING

YOU COULD DIE LAUGHING! 87

Lucinda - nightclothes, robe, house shoes
Colleen - nightgown, house shoes
Antonio - loud boxer shorts, t-shirt, white socks
Corky - pajamas
Zowie - nightclothes, house shoes
Helena - nightclothes, house shoes
Sammy - nightclothes, house shoes
Paulette - nightclothes, house shoes
Joey - expensive pajamas, silk robe, house shoes
Susan - nightclothes, robe, house shoes
Dexter - Western outfit
Stanley - Western outfit

Also By

Billy St. John

THE ABDUCTION
CINDY ELLA'S GOING TO THE BALL, BABY!
IS THERE A COMIC IN THE HOUSE?
THE PLOT, LIKE GRAVY, THICKENS
THE REUNION
THE WEREWOLF'S CURSE

SAMUELFRENCH.COM

www.ingramcontent.com/pod-product-compliance
Lightning Source LLC
Chambersburg PA
CBHW070647300426
44111CB00013B/2299